THE *ALMOST* UNPUBLISHED LENNY BRUCE

From the private collection of Kitty Bruce

RUNNING PRESS
Philadelphia, Pennsylvania

Acknowledgments

Our special gratitude to Mr. Studs Terkel and Mr. Paul Krassner for their help and gracious cooperation. Grateful acknowledgment is also made to the following for permission to reprint various materials in this book:

Photographs on pages 107, 108, 118, and 123 courtesy of United Press International, Inc.

"Bruce—He Knows Law, Law Knows Him," by Gail Cottman, originally appeared in *College Times*, published at California State University at Los Angeles.

"An Obituary" by Ralph J. Gleason originally appeared in *The San Francisco Chronicle* in somewhat different form.

"Non-Malignant Humor: An Impolite Interview," "On the Great Debate," "Letter From a Soldier's Wife," "The Great Hotel Robbery," "On George Lincoln Rockwell," "Stream of Consciousness," "Obscenity, Narcotics, and Me," and "The Fecalphiles" originally appeared in *The Realist*. Copyright 1959 through 1964 by The Realist Association, Inc.

"In the Beginning," "The Violent Liberals," "The Money I'm Stealing," "When in Doubt, Lie Like Hell," "Now See What You've Done? You've Lost My Place!," "Snobbery Small Talk," and "Mr. Clean" originally appeared in *Rogue* Magazine, published by Greenleaf Publishing Company, Evanston, Illinois.

Every effort has been made to respect the copyright rights of persons in the materials published herein. In some instances, despite every effort, the publisher has been unable to contact either persons who originally published some of the material or their successors in interest.

9 8 7 6 5 4 3 2 1
The digit on the right indicates the number of this printing.
Library of Congress Cataloging in Publication Data: Main entry under title: The unpublished Lenny Bruce. 1. Bruce, Lenny. 2. Comedians—United States—Biography. I. Bruce, Kitty. PN2287. B726A77 1984 792.7′028′0924 84-2034
ISBN: 0-89471-259-4 (paperback). ISBN: 0-89471-260-8 (library binding). Cover design by Toby Schmidt. Typography by CompArt and rci, Philadelphia, Pennsylvania. This book may be ordered by mail from the publisher. Please include 75 cents postage. But try your bookstore first. Running Press Book Publishers, 125 South 22nd Street, Philadelphia, Pennsylvania 19103.

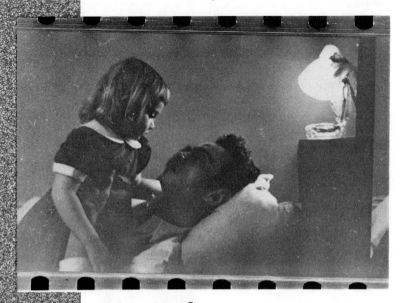

Foreword

When people remember those closest to them, they often think back on the effect that one person had on their particular life.

In retrospect, my father had so much effect on so many that it is difficult to put him in perspective when thinking about him. His efforts to fight for his own beliefs, or maybe just against the quizzical idea of being told "No"—I can't be sure which—caused a restless fire to burn within the man's very soul. But what I am sure of is that as a "whole man," father, son, husband, and friend, he believed, loved, cared, and fought within himself for what he thought was just.

I hope these pages and pieces of his life and works you are about to discover will lend a different side of "Lenny" to the ones who know him. And to the ones who don't, you are now being lovingly introduced to the unpublished Lenny Bruce.

—Kitty Bruce
March, 1984
New York City

In loving
memory of
Ralph J. Gleason
(1917-1975)

With special
thanks to
Steve Diamond,
Jean Gleason,
and Gloria Stavers

Contents

In The Beginning

When I was a boy, one of my favorite hiding places was under the sink, where I used to sit picking at the ripped linoleum and sort of half-staring at my Aunt's Private Business, which stood next to the vigilant CN bottle. (At this tender age I knew nothing of feminine hygiene; the only way I could differentiate between men and women at the time was women always had headaches and they didn't like whistling or cap guns.) I never knew what the hell it was for, all I knew was that it was none of my business. When you're eight years old, nothing is "any of your business."

Mema—that's my Aunt's name in Jewish—would sit rocking and twisting her handkerchief, peering through the faded tintex curtains, making a noise with her nose that I could never describe but I can still hear. She would rock and exclaim: "It's none of your business," "You know too much already," "You better go outside." My Aunt's fear of my becoming a pre-teen degenerate was responsible for my getting more fresh air than any child in the neighborhood.

"You're asking for it" would be a direct cue for my exit from under the sink. I would usually motivate this request with questions such as "Why do the hairs come out of your mole and nowhere else on your face?"

My second retreat was the porch or rather under the porch. Long Island in 1935 had lots of porches—porches and screen doors. Screen doors to push your nose against and porches to hide under. It always smelled funny under the porch, the dirt had a certain smell. I always had fantasies of finding the Lindbergh kidnap money which I would spend nobly on my Mother and Aunt, but not till they confessed about the under-the-sink apparatus.

I would usually hide under the porch until it came time to "get it." I would "get it" every night. "Wait till your Father comes home, then you're gonna get it." I

7

always thought what a pain in the ass it would be to be a Father. You have to work hard all day, and then instead of resting you have to give it to someone as soon as you come home because somebody's gotta "get it."

"I don't know what we're going to do with him. He was so fresh to Mema, you know what he asked?" and then they would all laugh and really get hysterical. After the laughter subsided I would get *schlepped* from under the porch, sometimes catching my corduroy knickers on a nail and then really get the crap whacked out of me—not for being fresh to Mema but for forgetting to change my good clothes after school.

Now when I look back in tender anger, I can hear the muffled voices through the kerosene stove, through the gray painted porch and the damp newspapers that waited tied up on the porch for the "Goodwill" that never picked up anything we gave them because we never had it packed right.

Pleasures were simple back then. I used to love to whistle and the first tune I learned by heart was *Amapola*. "Amapola, you pretty little poppy—" I was enthralled with the discovery of the jukebox. It was a wondrous marriage of music, science, light, and color. And now that I think of it, how delightful—a machine invented for fun, not for the tedious task of sewing, drilling, boiling, or killing, no staid contribution to science, just fun.

I received most of my musical education from the sounds that wafted from Angelo's Alley. *Angelo's Bar and Grill, Ladies Invited*. Moneywise, I always made a pretty good score in back of Angelo's. There would always be some deposit bottles, but the only difficulty was that you could never cash the bottles anywhere. Hoffman Ginger Ale bottles were really a prize, but Mr. Margolis, the grocer, had a slight sadistic streak in him and hated to cash deposit bottles. He used to ask, "Did you buy them here?" which was his sick little game since he cashed my Mother's relief check and knew we had no money to buy anything but staples. I would always fall prey to his Serge Rubinstein tactics and say, "Yes, I think we bought them here." Then he would fingersnap me in the back of my head as if he were thumping a melon. "Get the hell out of here, you never bought any soda, and if I hear of it, I'll report your Mother to the NRA man and have them take your check away."

I would really "get it" then. I could just hear the NRA man telling Mema, "Your nephew—you know, the one who knows too much already—has been arrested on a deposit bottle charge, so we have to take your relief check away."

That was the Big Threat of the day, taking the check away. The Goyim were always being threatened because of their presence in the bars and the Yidden for their presence in the banks.

Borden's milk bottles brought five cents apiece but the manager of the King Kullen Market would always stare at me as I swore, with no apparent guile, that I bought them yesterday and didn't know how the hell the dirt and cobwebs got inside.

For four bottles I would get twenty cents. I would spend twelve of it on a jar of Vaseline for Mema—she ate it by the ton. In later years I always meant to ask my doctor, Maurice Siegal, if there were any such thing as a Vaseline addict. To Mema, Vaseline was Jewish penicillin—she would rub it on anything. With a nickel of the change I would buy my Mother a *Liberty* Magazine. She liked them because the reading time was quoted, like "4 minutes, 30 seconds." She used to clock herself, and her chief aim was to beat the reading time, which she always succeeded in doing, but I am not sure she ever knew what the hell she read. "Vox Populi" was all I remember about that magazine.

With the remaining three cents I would usually buy a Guess What, a Mary Jane, and a Hooten. I would relish it when those candy days fell on the same days when we would have codfish cakes for supper. I hated codfish cakes, and turkey croquettes—that vile antecedent of the TV dinner—that looked like a Goyisha upside-down ice cream cone. The croquettes weren't bad enough but when that library paste gravy was added to it, it really became perdition.

Perhaps at this time I should offer explanations to readers who may misinterpret my phraseology as bigoted and perhaps limited at times. Unfortunately, my English literature background *is* limited and my conversation—spoken and written—is usually saturated with the argot of the hipster, the underworld, and Yiddishisms in the literate sense (as literate as Yiddish can be, since it is not a formal language).

"Goyish" means Christian but that is not the way I mean to use it. To me, if you live in New York or any major city, you are Jewish—doesn't matter if you're Catholic or Italian or what have you—you're Jewish if you live in New York. But if you live in Butte, Montana, you're Goyish even if you're Jewish. In other words, evaporated milk is Goyish even if the Jews invented it. Chocolate is Jewish and fudge is Goyish, Spam is Goyish and rye bread is Jewish, etc.

I have been very close to the analyst's couch many times; however, I think I have it whipped (if I could only stop thinking of whipping). My basic problem stems from my guilts about being a bad boy. My Mother and Father have been fanatically devoted to me all my life, but their devoted fanaticism is dwarfed by their addiction to Judaism. They are devout Orthodox Jews. This has been a big divider between my parents and myself for years. They are in their twilight years now, and I realize, according to their standards, the disgrace and humiliation I must have caused them.

I refused to become *Bar mitzvah.* I disgraced the rabbinical teacher by disclosing the fact that he was an out-and-out nut who used to expose himself on the subway platform at 59th Street in Brooklyn during the rush hour. He used to flash just before the doors closed. I never told anyone but him, so we made a deal. He told my parents that I couldn't learn and that I had a demoralizing effect on the other children. I heard, years later, that his career had been cut short when someone had shoved him at an inopportune time as the doors closed.

Getting back to being Jewish, my Father didn't give up, however; he drilled me with the Talmud, daily. Things were looking brighter until I fell in love with a girl—horror of horrors—who wasn't Jewish. But I thought the fact that her Father was a Doctor would soothe my family. He was the only colored doctor in Freeport, Long Island.

When I brought Rebecca and her Father over to the house for dinner at my Mother's suggestion (*"Nu, so bring Beckie and her Totta over and I'll make a kigel"*), I forgot that I hadn't mentioned what nationality they were . . . it didn't seem to matter. When my Mother answered the door, the Doc introduced himself. My Mother turned a darker shade than Beckie and the Doctor. These incidents seem to add up. I never saw Beckie after that. But now that my parents are going down the home stretch, I am really trying to be Jewish.

At Christmastime, for me, being Jewish is uncomfortable. Although it was over two thousand years ago, people still talk about it, and some people with a macabre sense of vigilante justice never quite have forgiven us. Let me tell you very candidly, I have read the life of Christ many times. I have read the Bible many times, and if Christ were alive today, I would devote my life to him. He represents all the truths and beauty. Most of all, he was an educator; a teacher. That's why it amazes me to see anyone in a synagogue or church who is not an out-and-out integrationist. If they are not, they are definitely anti-Christ.

Think about that last sentence awhile.

Let's leave the heavy aspect for a moment. I really have to check myself occasionally so that I don't get too philosophical. That's what gets me sick. Incidentally, I learned that the statement which made *Time* Magazine decide that I was the "sickest" was in regard to Loeb and Leopold. I said: "If Nathan Leopold had had any sense of humor, he would have grabbed another kid the day he got out."

For a while, and it's still prevalent, mention of Jews or being Jewish was a sticky subject. Miami Beach, which is at least 75 percent Jewish during the season, is so sick that owners who are Jewish request the performers, who are usually Jewish, "not to work so Jewish. The people want to get away from that."

Well, fortunately, by some twist of Fate, it's becoming *in* to be Jewish. Sammy Davis, Jr., started it and now all the hippies dig it . . . Even Baby Doll Carroll Baker and Elizabeth Taylor. Even the Vikings were Jewish: Tony Curtis and Kirk Douglas. The only Gentile was Ernest Borgnine, and he got killed. To quote one of the most brilliant comedians of all time, Irwin Corey, "I play Jewish chess. We use rabbis instead of bishops." Seriously, though, even the best-sellers in books are Jewish, such as *Exodus* and *Only In America*. And the best Broadway shows like Paddy Chayefsky's *Tenth Man* are Jewish.

The capper is a Jewish repertory company in Los Angeles that did a Yiddish version of *My Fair Lady*. A *YIDDISH My Fair Lady!* I can't wait to see it. I know I'll flip when I hear Eliza Doolittle's old man sing, "Get Me to the Shul on Time."

Letter from a Soldier's Wife

Who remembers? Who can I pester—God? Of course. He had a kid of His own. He spent a lot of time at the wailing post, as the Father, the Son, and the Holy Ghost, but still, He was never a mother. Only a mother knows what it is to lose a son in the service. And only a wife knows what it is to lose her husband.

It's getting near the time that will introduce the most dreaded aspect of The Emily Post Guide to Etiquette—the chapter on "Proper Garments for Funerals." How does one dress? Who will zip me up? Kiss my back after I'm snapped? It's not too late, God; there is still time to save him from being stilled. Time to save the most truthful—the strongest—man in the world.

You don't believe? Just ask my children. He was a soldier that stood quiet and obedient, not as spectacular as the one that dropped his bomb over Hiroshima, that burned the lids away from the skil-

lion almond eyes that will never know the blessing the Japanese sandman has to offer.

Don't take away those arms that soothe me as a poultice. How obsolete the other pillow becomes, except to hug, and smother Your convulsive beckoning to the dead. What can I tell you? How can I single out one good deed, so that You will enforce the Fifth Commandment? Thou Shalt Not Kill! Please, Jehovah, just get to the masses with one little miracle, one carnival-like trick—sky-write, spell it out in lightning: THOU SHALT NOT KILL. Punctuate it with thunderclaps. Show me strength, show me the sky is Yours. Please, dear God, save my man's life. I'm sure your Son would approve.

Very truly yours,
Mrs. Adolf Eichmann

LETTERS TO WILLIAM HAMLING, PUBLISHER OF "ROGUE" MAGAZINE

ROGUE MAGAZINE, EVANSTON, ILL—FEB 8 TO BILL HAMLING.
   DEAR BILL: CALL ME FEB 9TH URGENT 6:00 P.M. MIAMI TIME URGENT

                                                LENNY BRUCE

ROGUE MAGAZINE, EVANSTON, ILL—FEB 9 TO BILL HAMLING.
   URGENT DEAR BILL: IGNORE LAST TELEGRAM

                                                LENNY BRUCE

                                            March 15

Dear Bill:—
   I cancelled the call I had to you because I felt it was too close to our deadline to make any demands. Incidentally, I particularly liked Alfred Bester [who wrote a monthly column about Broadway]. Hentoff is always good, and Harlan's thing was a gas.
   BUT...
   What is it with your quote beautiful girls unquote? I have seen fags swinginger-looking than your center chick. Where is it you get these Woolworth waitresses?

                                              Your friend,
                                            Lenny

                                            March 20

Dear Bill:—
   Sure I like the magazine, it is only that I see so many beautiful dolls around it amazes me why you pick the ones you do. But anyone who would let that elderly woman pose as a Miami U. co-ed has an adventuresome spirit, I give you that.

                                              Your friend,
                                            Lenny

                                            April 16

Dear Bill:—
   Enclosed are some slides taken by a very good friend of mine, and I have promised him that you will pay him top dollar and upon acceptance, you will send him a check immediately and a letter telling him he is a "good boy" and "Where the hell have you been all this time?" and "You should see the crap the other guys send me" and all those other methods used in coolie labor exploitation.
   Now, if you decide to turn the pictures down, you will return them immediately to the Beverly Hills address, and I shall think nothing of it. The fact that you shall never see your kids again has nothing to do with me. Also, I do not have to remind you that many magazine factories have recently burned to the ground mysteriously.

                                              Your friend,
                                            Lenny

                                            June 9

Dear Bill:—
   To be serious for once, enclosed are some shots of Miami—the chic hotels, plus the other side that not too many people touch upon: the pensioners, the silent armies who sit and wait. Our "senior citizens"—the Moms and Dads who are in the way and have been sent south to retire in the sunshine and hustle candy bars for their room and board.
   Just the same, they are very happy, very spirited. They sing and have fun on the beach. I joined them, and Dave photographed them. While the bigger hotels charge $50 a day during the season, the pensioners can enjoy the same beautiful sunshine and velvet tropical weather for approximately $900 a year.

                                              Your friend,
                                            Lenny

The Violent Liberals

The papers have been full of it. "150,000 STUDENT RIOTERS FORCE IKE TO CANCEL TOKYO TRIP." "NIXON STONED IN SOUTH AMERICA BY PROTESTING STUDENTS." Protesting against the immoral, the anti-Gideon act of killing Chessman; protesting the cliché "Regardless of race, color or creed . . ."

Students weeping because the Barton MacLane, Jimmy Cagney image of the U.S. has been shattered. "Soon I'll be outta stir and then what'll I do?" and Pat O'Brien would answer, "In our country, once a man pays for his crimes he has paid his debt in full and he has a chance again." Do you hear that, Albert Maltz, Dalton Trumbo, Robert Oppenheimer? You've paid your debt to society and we'd like to forgive you, only James Cagney is now Bill Halsey in the Navy and Barton MacLane is dead . . .

That's the immediate picture. Now add a few touches here and there for the benefit of the vast majority of the world's peoples who consider themselves the colored races. Think of young, black Mac Parker, who was dragged from a cell in Poplar, Mississippi last year and murdered by White Supremacy. A man was murdered in the United States of America, and the Grand Jury met and closed the case!

Look through the Aeroflex. The picture is in sharp focus. The Tokyo rioters are the sweet, intellectual good guys, and the Eisenhower Administration is the bad guy. But let's get objective and pull back the camera to a nice, wide angle and realize that those students are full of crap, too. For if they had had any Christian compassion, they would have kissed Haggerty and they would have embraced Eisenhower. And the South Americans certainly didn't project any Christian attitude by stoning Nixon.

The popular consensus is that we beat up the Japs after they attacked us first so now they've got a goddamned nerve. Actually they haven't. Not if you believe Pat O'Brien and I certainly do. How long must one repay? (Maybe Eisenhower could have saved face by visiting the Japanese nude show in Vegas as a token gesture.) It has come to pass that we're actually living a fantasy. It's group against group, and certainly it's no great profundity to tell you that there are no good guys, no bad guys.

Here's the trend: It's been chic for a long time for liberals to identify with Stevenson and hate Nixon, for example. But how liberal are they if they cannot be liberal with Nixon? Truth comes to all of us at different degrees and levels; those we love and those we hate are actually a part of us. Every reader knows, if he searches his soul, that he is part McCarthy, part Stevenson, part Khrushchev, every antithesis combined. And, knowing this, you will hate sometimes. I will hate, have hated, and will continue hating. But I have come to the realization that I am certainly not superior to those I hate.

Time has a great deal to do with our sense of values. Nelson Rockefeller, the Governor of New York, is a contemporary man equally at home with Monet or the works of Nelson Algren. And yet, at the turn of the century, the name of Rockefeller aroused nothing but contempt in people. "That senile old S.O.B. in his knickers giving those goddamned dimes away."

Today the man who is long and thin and lean in his continental suit is a sexual image. It is hip to be thin and lean. Now—remember the ad in the old magazines? A skinny, ninety-pound weakling and a voluptuous girl and a beach ball lie on a blanket. The bully passes, kicking sand in the weakling's face, and walks off with the girl, leaving our hero alone with the beach ball. But in ninety days Charles Atlas could give him a body like his. And then the ninety-pound weakling would be big and beefy like Charles Atlas, who would certainly have a tough time making out today.

I have spent three decades observing the decadence. Although the decadence I view mirrors the corruptness in myself, I have not adopted the puerile attitude of Norman Vincent Peale, whose words in print are blurred and obscured by drooling sentimentality.

To tie it up, has Eisenhower and his Administration been corrupt? No. Has Eisenhower and his Administration purposely done damage to the country? No. Eisenhower and his Administration are not mean, corrupt men—they are merely inadequate men who have proven their lack of leadership by popularizing the phrase "Yankee Go Home!"

I don't want to hear any explanations—it's too late for that. Americans are not liked anywhere in the world for the first time in our history, except possibly in Manila, where we are loved. But the Filipinos who screamed "We Like Ike" would certainly be shocked if they were to visit Eisenhower on the cruiser *St. Paul* and see his Filipino friends in white jackets waiting on him.

I abhor Communism—since it upholds the philosophy of violence. But as a good American, I would certainly feel hypocritical if, in my own country, sixth-generation Americans cannot sit at lunch counters or have trouble going to school. It is my country, I love it, I will fight for it, but when it is wrong, I will admit it. But there is no point, God knows, in embracing the corrupt, sickening philosophy of "An eye for an eye."

AN INTERVIEW
WITH
STUDS
TERKEL

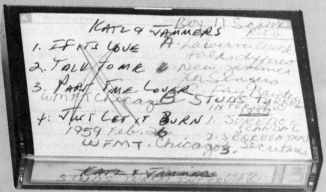

Broadcast February 26, 1959 on Radio Station WFMT in Chicago

Studs Terkel: Sitting across the microphone is one of the most deft comics of the year . . .

Lenny Bruce: What?

ST: . . .Perhaps one of the most irreverent of comics, Lenny Bruce . . .

LB: Deaf?

ST: No, *deft*—who is now appearing at the Cloisters. I think the comedy of Lenny Bruce has to be seen as well as heard. In hearing him, you dig what the man is saying, and it is a great deal, too. Sometimes a comic can say more through his sharp, barbed wit than a platform speaker who says little, really. But Lenny Bruce, before we try to dig the nature of your comedy, that which is described as sick humor—before we touch that, let's get down to fundamentals. What would you say comprises a comedian? What makes a comedian an effective comic?

LB: Well, that actually borders on semantics. My concept of a comedian is an individual who creates his own material, a guy who's got a funny bone. I believe that there are very few comedians. There are a lot of good comedy *actors.* Now, I'll give you an example—Buddy Hackett's Chinese waiter routine. Have you seen him do that?

ST: Very funny.

LB: It is very funny! Now, he created that and performs it very well, and it's a screamingly funny bit. Now let's take that Chinese waiter and give it to William Powell, to Robert Cummings, or Cary Grant; to any number of fine comedy actors. We'll rehearse them for two or three weeks, and they'll do the bit and get screams— just the same screams that Buddy Hackett will get with it. But that does not make them comedians.

ST: In other words, then, this is just a routine—a sketch, let's say—that is not innate in the man himself. You think this is just a routine that anyone could do, really?

LB: Oh, definitely. Any good comedy actor. But the comedian is the guy who can create. Mort Sahl is creative. He makes up the joke and then performs it. Jonathan Winters is really a comedian. Buddy Hackett is a comedian.

ST: Where does this leave the stand-up comics, quote unquote, who have stables of writers?

LB: They are fine comedy actors. For example, George Gobel is a fine comedy actor. Red Buttons is a fine comedy actor. Dick Shawn is a fine comedy actor.

ST: You say these people, then, are creatures of their writing?

LB: Yes, but I don't mean that "creatures" facetiously, to sound like they are nothing. They are excellent, wonderful performers, but they are not comedians.

ST: A comedian is a self-sufficient type whose material is his own?

LB: A guy who thinks funny. His mind is working, and he thinks on his feet and swings.

ST: But you are different—a comedian in the general category of Mort Sahl. That is, you comment on the contemporary scene, don't you?

LB: Yes, but I don't think I'm anything like Mort at all. Another fellow who commented on the passing scene was Henry Morgan, and yet I feel nothing like Morgan, or—let's see, who else?

ST: Am I right in saying this? The only similarity is that you comment on the current scene. The key difference between you and a man like Sahl or Morgan, let's say, is that they comment from the outside looking in. But you are a participant. You do all the voices; you become the various characters.

LB: Yes, I do use the facets of theater. Now if Mort or Henry Morgan or Berle—Berle's a good example. If Johnny Ray is popular, Berle will do a joke; he'll say, "Well, I don't have to do this for a living. I could be selling Kleenexes to Johnny Ray," right? But he won't do Johnny Ray crying. We'll take the jukebox scandal now. Mort or Berle or a stand-up monologist will say, "I don't have to do this for a living. I could be selling bulletproof vests to the jukebox operators."

See, now that would be commenting on the passing scene. Myself, I'll do characters, you know; I'll do a bit instead of just commenting. I'll actually get into the bit—attack the satire, perhaps in this way:

Back during the war, it was very easy to sell merchandise. Then, salesmen were called just plain order-takers. But now, in the post-war period, the individual has to really get out and hard-sell. Now, we find two salesmen in the record industry approaching a prospective buyer. We hear them knocking at the door. *[Knock, knock, knock.]*

[In a Japanese-accented voice:] "Come in?"

[In a gangster voice:] "Hello, we're here to sell you some albums. My name is Nunzio Flaherty, and this is Mr. Martin here. We've got some wonderful albums we'd like you to buy."

"Well, we don't have any calls for record albums."

"That's all right. You'll be the first Japanese restaurant that handles them."

"Well . . . [flustered] What kind of records are they?"

"You'll love them. One's called *Remember Pearl Harbor*, and the other's *The Bridge on the River Kwai*."

"Well, I don't know. I'll have to talk to my partner about this."

"We already straightened it out with him—five minutes before he passed away. You understand?"

"Well, how much are the records?"

"They're $8.95 an album. We'll let you off easy. We'll start you off with five thousand."

"These are nice albums, but wait a minute, where's the records?"

"Never mind that, buster. See how the albums do first."

Et cetera, et cetera. And that's how I usually attack a satire.

ST: This attack, though, is so sharp. It seems more effective. This is not to put down—to use your jazz terminology—the other comedians, but in becoming these figures, you make it so much more vivid for the viewer.

LB: Yes, and I also think that they know it is satire for satire's sake. With the exception of a very few situations, I have no messages. Some, actually, I feel very strongly about and I'll discuss them with you. But I have no political leanings whatsoever. And when I do a satire, it'll just be fun for fun's sake. The only things that I feel very strongly about—and I'll attack them through satire—are some principles of American heritage that I'm very proud of, and things that I think we're losing sight of, such as integration—which I'm very interested in and feel is very important.

Before I'll do it satirically, I explain to the audience that integration—if you want to attack it from a logical standpoint—is very important just for the sake of education. And I'll explain that we have a very large Negro population in this country, and if we don't educate them, we're in serious trouble. We have to have education, that's obvious. Then I hit them from a pure logic standpoint. If you don't want to integrate people, all right. But you cannot have the nerve to charge them income tax or draft them in the Army. That's ridiculous. How can you tax people and draft them and ask them to obey the laws and not give them their equal rights? It makes no sense.

And then, further, I'll attack it from a religious standpoint, which is the most important and usually the most powerful argument. If you are a Christian or a Jew and you believe in the Bible, in its principles, you cannot really call yourself a good Christian or a good Jew and not wholeheartedly believe in integration. Because I know that Christ or Moses could never, ever tell a child that he couldn't go to school. He could never, ever say to a child, "You can't drink out of that fountain, that's a white fountain." 'Cause I know Christ or Moses could never make anybody cry or hurt their feelings. So by not wholeheartedly believing in integration, you're not a Christian.

And *then* I will go on to satirize and get sort of a humorous thing going. I will say, "Now, I'll take you to the home of Governor Faubus. The Governor will be played by various and sundry characters. We find the Governor talking to his daughter, and the daughter says . . .

17

[Southern accent:] "Well, Daddy, I've got a wonderful surprise for you."

[Southern male voice:] "Well, what is it, Belle of the South?"

"Well, Daddy, your daughter Sheila Joy is going to get married."

"Married! Well, well, that certainly brings a warm spot to my old Southern heart. I can't believe you're such a big girl, Sheila. Are you marrying a local boy?"

"No, Daddy. He's a New York stage actor. Mom and I met him last year in Syosset, Long Island."

"Well, I've never had too much truck with stage folk. But I'm sure if my daughter Sheila Joy picked him out, he's a fine, upstanding man. What's his name, Sugar?"

"Harry Belafonte."

"Hmmm, an Italian boy, eh? Well, that's wonderful, Sheila."

And et cetera, et cetera.

ST: And so you caricature the whole situation.

LB: Yes. I've gotten the message across, and I won't go out of it heavy. I'll go out of it light and humorous.

ST: You are a comedian with a point of view. Sometimes a thinking entertainer is considered a dangerous entertainer. But you feel that point of view is an important part of your comedy?

LB: Yes, and I feel every individual is different, and that you can't really generalize. Here's the way I feel about it, actually: I'll never cram anything down anybody's throat.

I would never be working today if I had an agent. I've had agents for very short periods of time, and they've been a detriment. Now this routine, for example, or any routine I do—an agent would say, "That's poison! We could never book him anywhere. That's ridiculous, you know. There'll be too much conflict." But what has happened is that I get continual acceptance, which sounds very braggadocio. But I never—it's very seldom that I ever—do a mis-show. This consistency with repeat business during the week is rather fine. People come back, bring two of their friends, and they can't argue with that kind of acceptance.

ST: You feel, then, you can do much more with a broad audience that covers—

LB: Yes, the show-biz mind is very narrow. The average comedian and theatrical agent are in a very small orbit. They usually refer to audiences as *they*. "They" won't dig this, "they" won't dig that. And I'm so fed up with the trite, "Well, in New York they'll dig it, but in Davenport, Iowa. . . ." You know, they're busy worrying about Davenport, Iowa or Fayetteville, Arkansas; and little do they realize that *they* are no longer "they."

You can't generalize. They're pretty hip in Fayetteville, Arkansas and pretty hip in Davenport, Iowa; and the people who are really the geniuses—the Hidden Persuaders, the Vance Packards—realize this. The greatest proof is that the big, best-selling cigarettes don't advertise differently for Davenport, Iowa or Belmont, Long Island. They would, immediately, if they thought they're different—but they're not. People are basically all the same, with the same drives. The same people get divorced, the same people cry and have babies and other clichés.

ST: And the show-biz agent, quote unquote, is more provincial than the

Iowan he's putting down.

LB: Actually, it's the truth.

ST: Well, on this point of the audience becoming more hip, Herb Caen, who is from *The San Francisco Chronicle*, made a comment about you that was quoted in the newest issue of *Playboy*, "The Rebel with a Caustic Cause." Does this really hit you? ". . . Audiences, however, are growing hipper, and the inside comic is the order of the day. Lenny Bruce is just a little more inside than any other comedian working . . . He is a rebel, but not without a cause, for there are shirts that need unstuffing, egos that need deflating, and precious few people to do this sticky job with talent and style. Sometimes you feel a twinge of guilt for laughing at one of Lenny's mordant jabs—but that disappears a second later when your inner voice tells you, with pleased surprise, 'But that's true.' The kind of truth that might not have dawned on you if there weren't a few Lenny Bruces around to hammer it home."

You feel this touches what you're trying to do?

LB: Actually, it's very flattering. It makes me feel very good. I pay all these guys off—I give them a bottle of Scotch. No, that was very kind of him, and that's actually the way I feel. They say that I am far out, and I feel as Ralph Gleason said: "Far out depends on where you are standing."

ST: Let me just explain: Ralph Gleason is a jazz critic who's a very perceptive man in many fields.

LB: And actually responsible, I would say, for my first thrust, the actual getting out there. He was the first columnist—he's syndicated—who really got out and said, "This guy is good."

ST: I like what Gleason says in the liner notes to your album. He compares you to a good jazz musician: "Bruce's comedy is a dissent from a world gone mad." And now we're coming to his matter. Your humor has been described as sick humor. How do you feel about that particular adjective, that appellation?

LB: I feel "sick" is just a nebulous word, just a hack-writer kind of thing. They like comparisons, the same as you'll ask a guy, "What's the Beat Generation? What's 'beat'?" and they'll just say a word they found. It's sort of commercial now to hang onto "sick." In the *Sick Humor* album Ralph refers to me as the most jazz-oriented comic, which is very gratifying.

ST: Why would he say, "A social commentator as jazz musician is Lenny Bruce. An interesting source of speculation is why his comedy of dissent has flourished in jazz clubs"? Why would you say it has, Lenny?

LB: Well, I don't like to be a martyr, you know, and say, "I'm this, that, or the other thing." But I feel the biggest successes are because they're something different. People appreciate that originality, and will go out and see it, even if they don't like it. They'll say, "Well, let's go see what he's doing."

ST: What about your form? I mean, does this put you close to a jazz musician, the fact that your routine is not verbatim?

LB: No, that's what he said. He says, "He terrifies other comedians, the usual ones, by his material, in the same way the jazz musician terrifies the hotel bands and the Mickey Mouse tenor."

ST: You improvise a great deal?

LB: Uh-huh. Everything that I do, I've created. I've been in the industry ten years, actually working as a comic about five years. And I've probably created around seven hours of material. The laughs in seven hours go—[snaps his fingers]—you know, there are a lot of laughs. I don't actually sit down and write out a routine. I'll ad-lib it on the floor, but line by line, and eventually, it'll snowball into a bit. I'll never actually do the same routine twice. I'll do a routine awhile, then I'll get bored with it, then I'll do another thing. I'll develop probably about a new three or four minutes a week.

ST: So the element of freshness is always there, as though we ourselves are seeing creativity. In a sense, your humor—though described as sick, which you call a cliché term—probably is reaffirmative, because what you're kidding is the phoniness of the day.

LB: Yes.

ST: You're not a negative guy, really. The fact is, you have a viewpoint that's positive.

LB: Yeah, and I feel that "sick" is just a commercial word.

ST: There's something you were about to say earlier about the low rating of audiences, which may lead into the field of television itself, the biggest field of mass communication.

LB: I feel there's a big problem in the industry today. People are always screaming about bad television, bad this or that, and I don't think anyone has ever approached this facet: Secretaries are very bad, outer-office people who become monsters.

Now this is sort of weird. You'll get a guy, a writer—we'll say a song-writer, a very sensitive guy—and he's written a tune. Now he goes and he's got the song. . . .

[Mocking voice:] "Who do you want to see?"

"I'd like to see Mr. Anderson."

"Do you have an appointment?"

"No, but I'd like to see him. I've got a tune here."

"Well, you have to make blah, blah, blah . . ."

Now usually, any artist who is good usually is very sensitive, a pretty insecure guy, and that's why he writes something pretty nice and pretty sensitive. This kind of guy can't stand that sort of brash rejection. So consequently, when she goes, "Blah, blah, blah, and you'll have to wait," the guy just feels so brought down, you know? He can't take the rejection. He'll either go back home and get juiced, or get high or get out of his nut, and think, "Oh, I'm not going to go back." Meanwhile, the brash guy with a lot of moxie, with the stick-to-it-ness—he'll stay there, he'll sit in the outer office. He'll make it. Finally the material will get through, but it'll probably be second-rate. Meanwhile, the guy who has some sensitivity, his stuff will never be seen. If big agencies only knew how little sensitivity many secretaries have, even on phones! They'll just keep you hanging. Nothing can bring a guy down more. You know, you'll call some cat, and he's in conference.

ST: Well, this is an explanation we haven't heard till now.

LB: Yes, it really brings you down. You yourself have probably waited sometime—instead of the secretaries saying, "Sit here," and maybe talking to you a little and making you feel a little relaxed, they've such a militant attitude.

ST: The fact that you—obviously a sensitive comedian—are scoring is a happy sign, I think.

LB: Well, I never scored with any of the secretaries, if that's what you're inferring.

ST: If we may just plug—more than a plug, we should suggest very strongly to the audience the album that you've put out for Fantasy. It's called *The Sick Humor of Lenny Bruce*, and there are six or seven different routines.

LB: Satires. There are some that could never be played on the air, anywhere.

ST: And yet excellent for the audience to hear at home and at parties. Fantasy LP 7001—is that this album?

LB: Yes, this is *Sick Humor*.

ST: Well, that's 7003. You have another album, 7001.

LB: Yes, that's *Interviews of Our Times*. But *The Sick Humor of Lenny Bruce* album, I'm the most proud of.

ST: You have another week.

LB: Week and a half.

ST: Week and a half. So I suggest you head down—head *up*, perhaps, to The Cloisters, at the Maryland Hotel, Rush and Delaware.

Miscellaneous Notes for Routines Performed in St. Louis and Chicago, September, 1959

On Krushchev's visit: I wish I could show him around, or maybe just let a cab driver show him around. Get him balled, juiced, loaded; forget the museums.

Ringsiders that have to look up at you: It's weird, you can almost look up into my nose. I have to pick my nose before I go on.

Judges who get a sexual satisfaction out of heavy sentences: "I give you twenty years—quick, give me my Kleenex."

Boy's Town's Father Flanagan: "Isn't that wonderful how my boys grow their own flowers—and they smoke them, too!"

I like Thom McAn shoes. I can't wear them out, but what I really like, they gave me a whistle when I bought these.

No use for letter H in Italian alphabet.

Forgetting subject I started on: That's weird; I'll probably think of it when I get home. Then I'll call you all up!

Cigarettes: How I got away from menthol cigs. My road manager, who is a real momzer, can't stand them. I used to smoke Salems, and he said to me one day, "So you're really going to smoke one of those Vicks-Salve-filled cigarettes?" After that, forget it! The very thought that the cigarette contained Vicks Salve sickened me. Imagine if it did. Can't you see people with a cold rubbing the cigarettes on their chest? Or sticking a filter-tip Salem in their nose and inhaling it? Ugh. Aaaah!!

Headline about man biting off woman's tongue (after imitating her way of talking): She is being booked for a poetry-in-jazz concert.

I can never kill a fly anymore without thinking I killed Vincent Price.

He has a strange haircut. He comes from a very wealthy family, and that's how the family got rich—they never spent any money on haircuts.

Routine on trying to take a girl out: Why can't you just say, "I want to be with you, hug, and kiss you"? No: "Come up while I change my shirt." Or coffee—"Let's have a cup of coffee." In fifty years, "coffee" will be another dirty word.

Some girls have a 38 bust, but the way they measure for a bust is weird. A girl could have a big back and be flat-chested and still be a 38.

If Governor Long is elected, that's it! I'm not going to pay my taxes or anything. I'm just going to lay down and wet the bed.

When you feel people have been to see another show: Oh, you were over to the Blah-Blah Club, seeing those old-timers out of respect, and now you're drunk and cranky.

Gene Krupa Story: How can we get people to believe how bad narcotics are when we glamorize it? Any teenager is going to try it when they've seen scenes like Frank Sinatra bawling, "Get on top of me, baby, I want to kick!"

Little Rock: They give the Negro a writing test. If he can write with a ballpoint pen on wax paper, he can enter school.

Bar stool: Shelley Berman made this in summer camp.

Why can you people afford to sit at the tables? Because you people have exploited the people who sit at the bars!

Who is the biggest Communist in the U.S.? A TV personality. A man who has more Russians on his show than anyone—Ed Sullivan.

Chinamen: The Chinese have been getting away with murder for years. They think they're smart, with their beady eyes—and they all look like they have hepatitis—sneaking around those laundries and restaurants for years, with that long fagalah hair hanging from the backs of their heads. They try to tell us that they never get into any trouble. And why not—all they do is sit around smoking that opium and making up those egg rolls.

Leaving stage: Unlike Chez Paree, I have to do good in this club. Because when I finish my work up here, I've got to walk through you.

I was really surprised when I found out who was behind Playboy Magazine—the Legion of Decency! Now, let me explain the function of the Legion of Decency. They censor objectionable, lewd, and lascivious books, motion pictures, and other art forms. The fact is, Playboy has money in it. I never expected to see Bishop Fulton Sheen in the centerfold! How it happened: years ago, Hugh Hefner, the Editor, helped out a small neighborhood church that was going bad—which is unusual, for a church to go bad. This place had a bad location and just depended on walk-by trade. Hugh got greedy and said, "Let's put in a little Bingo." That was all right, but when they put in the 26 girls, that did it!!

Audiences: First-show people sit there like it's New Year's Eve, with the hat and horn—"All right, make me laugh!" One thing about getting here at 6:00, you beat the men's room attendant.

Some people say, "Why be dirty?" Why? It gets me horny!

Chicago people have a strange way of talking—they're always looking for someone who isn't there.

Ted Lewis has opium in that clarinet. Sure, that's why he says, "Is everybody happy?"

Hawaiians: Now usually, you say, "Go back where you came from!" It's easy to say that to people who come from somewhere. But these people, they don't know where they came from, so how can you say, "Go back" to someone if they haven't come from somewhere?

Exposé on Big Crime: A candy store operator played by Mdme. Ouspenskaia. Voice: "Vee are tired of you rackvateers taking a penny from our halavah sale." And so her and the rest of the candy store women joined forces and moved to Calumet City and became hookers.

This is a good, solid drinking bar, the type of place where people know when it opens, know when it closes—and are there both times.

I repeat what I do because I have no confidence in this audience remembering anything.

This dog will kill you. It's the only trick he does. I pay a guy $50 to dress like a postman. I bite him and let the dog watch. He digs that!

Transcript of an Unidentified Live Performance

. . . What have I got here? Cancer! A.M.A. tells me that I get cancer smoking these, and I continue smoking them. This helps me be a little more liberal, 'cause no longer now can I point a finger at a drunk and tell him, "What's the matter with you, man? Aren't you using your brains? You keep drinking, and it's ruining your health, your family, your business—no brains, that's all!"

He's got a *lot* of brains. That has nothing to do with it. He's gonna keep drinking, and I'm gonna keep smoking. I've been thinking about what the ad companies are going to do. Well, they're not going to stop selling cigarettes. I can't knock them for that, 'cause everything is profit-motivation, so what are you gonna do, man? What they'll probably do, the ad companies, is make it hip to have cancer. They'll make cancer a status symbol in the community. They'll start with soft-sell advertisements, guys talking in two-minute spots, you know:

"Say, Bill, haven't seen you in a couple of years. You really look great!"

"Why shouldn't I? I've got cancer!"

"Are you kidding me, Bill? Well, that's terrible."

"Terrible the way *you* see it, not the way I see it. I was making about twenty-five hundred dollars a year selling shoes at home. Now since I got cancer—you never see any *schlub* with cancer! Who has it? Doctors, lawyers, and judges! So I started thinking at home, the rich people are keeping it away from us with those charity drives they have."

"And it's really good for you?"

"Certainly is."

"Well, that's wonderful! How do you get it?"

"Chesterfields!"

Now, of course you don't get cancer in Chesterfields. All cigarettes have it.

Filters are just a facade. . . .

I cannot indict *Time* Magazine, 'cause who is *Time* Magazine? Fifty million people who coordinate all together to make one magazine, right? So they send guys to interview me, you know, and the last write-up they gave me said, "He uses four-letter words as often as conjectures"—which is gross reporting, 'cause "*schmuck*" has six letters to it.

Now let's say they ask these questions and they get really personal with me. I will start to *schuck* with them, you know, and assume they'll know that I'm putting them on. But no, these cats are very legit! They'll say, "Are you married?"

"No, I'm divorced very happily."

"What happened to your marriage?"

So I think I'll throw a stock comic cliché line and they'll *know* it's a put-on: "My marriage was broken up by my mother-in-law."

"Oh, oh! Mother-in-law jokes! Write that down, that's funny: mother-in-law jokes. What happened?"

"Well, let's see. My mother-in-law broke up the marriage. One day my wife came home early from work, and she found us in bed together."

"What? Your mother-in-law in bed with you?"

"Yeah, that's right."

"Well, that's disgusting!"

"Oh, well, she was horny and she came on to me."

"With your *mother*? Well, that's psychotic!"

"Why? It was *her* mother, not mine."

"Oh, well, then it's all right, I guess."

By the way, I'm not proud that I'm divorced. It's a failure, you know, and it's a hangup, being divorced. Especially if you're on the road. Society has made up a lot of dirty words that actually hurt me as an individual.

Now, I'm on the road, and it's three o'clock in the morning, and I meet a girl, and I like her. Supposing I just have a record I wanted to hear, or I have a good painting, an original Degas—and I want to relate to her, just talk to her. There's no lust, no carnal image there. But because where I live is a dirty word— at three in the morning—I can't say to her, "Would you come to my hotel?" 'Cause *hotel* is a dirty word at three A.M. Not the next day at two o'clock in the afternoon when the Kiwanis meet there, though—then *hotel* is clean. But at three in the morning, Jim, that's it.

So you start to think. You know you can't say *hotel* to a chick, so you try to think of what won't offend. What is a clean word to society? *Trailer!* Trailers are hunting and fishing and outdoors. You tell a chick, "Hey, you wanna come to my trailer?" there's nothing dirty in that.

"Okay, uh, where is it?"

"Inside my hotel room. But it's right inside the door!"

Being in show business, every chick I meet—the first thing she hits you with is like, "Look, I dunno what kind of a girl you think I am, but I know you show people. You got all those broads down in the dressing room, and they're all ready for you."

"That's a lie. There's nobody down there."

"Never mind! I know you get all you want."

I *don't*. That's what everybody thinks, but I never make out. There's nobody in the dressing room. Every chick *thinks* that, but nothing happens. That's why Frank Sinatra never gets laid—it's hip not to ball him. Nobody does it to him but the old Swedish maid, who doesn't even know his name.

Women always have the image of those other women running around, but they're not. You're all virtuous. You're not unique because you don't ball, *none* of you do! It has to mean something to all of you. Listen, it doesn't have to mean something to me, it just feels good. Doesn't *that* mean anything to you?

No, no, it's really gotta mean something to me, I gotta meet somebody who'll mean something. That's it. Then I start to intellectualize, and I really miss out—all the time.

You get hung up. Every chick will say, like, "I'm not promiscuous like those other girls, and men pride themselves in not being promiscuous." Well, you are looking at a man who is promiscuous—when I'm allowed to be! 'Cause I like pretty faces. And I'm a complete narcissist, so if there's pretty chicks, man, I would swing every day if I were allowed to.

The average chick between thirty and fifty, who's divorced, always indicts her sister as promiscuous. I assume that the average woman between thirty and fifty who's divorced is intimate with about twenty-five strange guys a year, different guys. And they would deny this, until I would bring these twenty-five guys over to their house on the same afternoon. "Yes, it was a big year, and gee, I forgot Palm Springs . . . 'n' that night at the party when I was in the kitchen getting ice and that guy came in, and he gets really strange in that area . . ."

All right, so you meet a chick, you say, "Well, what'll I do?" Trailer? That's out. It's a perdition to pass the hotel desk. Then, if you're in the area where the chick has her own pad—but no! You can't go over to her house. 'Cause every chick I know between thirty and fifty, who's divorced, has a seven-year-old kid.

It's a prop! Yeah, they get this seven-year-old kid from Central Casting and bring him out so he's standing there. A lot of times, you go on the road and you meet waitresses. They're always scuffling, so they have a one-room pad. There's one bed, and you're always sitting on the kid's foot, you know:

"Will he wake up?"

"No, he's a sound sleeper."

"Hello, Uncle Fred!"

"Is he comfortable sleeping that way, with his knees in his mouth?"

Okay, the chick with some more bread has got a one-bedroom apartment. Quote the *Citizen News:* "ONE BEDR. APT. FOR RNT."—That's a contraction, there—"NO KIDS." So she's got no kids, right? But here's a hangup—she has a French poodle that wants to stay in the bedroom with you.

And you say, "Why doesn't the dog go out?"

"Aw, he's cute, he won't bother anybody."

"Yeah, but I—I dig him, but why don't he go outside?"

"He's a little dog. He's not gonna bother us."

"I *hope* he's not gonna join in with us. I'm just not that mature. I'm not an exhibitionist. I just can't go to the toilet with the door open, and the dog in the room is a hangup. So, uh—if you wanna tell him about it later, that's cool. But let him split now, all right?"

And that always alienates them. Then they get hungup with the dog; "You're separating me from the dog." You know, I got a whole thing about dogs. I really feel that God meant for animals to be in the forest, not locked up in your apartment. They're not comfortable there in a one-room pad. They're supposed to be running—what's their function in an apartment? Or in a home, man?

I am embarrassed at *anyone* kissing my hand. And for an animal to play dead is blasphemous. On top of that, I'm a fastidious nut. Siamese cats . . . I don't care if you clean that box, it's *there*. And they've got a weird dog—Cocker Spaniels. They're the ones that are spayed and have asthma, and they walk around going *hunnnhhh*. A Doberman Pinscher, at least there's a functional dog. You raise him, you train him—in ten years, he kills you.

So then, finally, you go to the *real* dirty word, which is even trite-dirty—motel! You tell the chick, "Well, let's go to a motel." That has a stigma to it, you know. There's no rationalization of motels. You almost have to be a machine to go there, because the glass is sanitized for your safety, the toilet seat's tied up, and the guy at the desk is always reading *The Watchtower*. There's no hallway, it's like, "Here we are in the room! . . . But what're we here for?" Oh God, don't say that! "Well, here we are, ha, ha, ha."

"What'll we do?"

"Read."

The architects are actually sadistic. They should figure out the motel differently. There is only one area, but at least make fake doors that don't go anywhere: one says "Kitchen." "Nursery"—*that* would be cooler, you know? . . .

On George Lincoln Rockwell

Friends of mine are always showing me articles—"Look at what this bigoted bastard wrote!" And then I dug something: Liberals will buy anything a bigot writes, and they really support it. George Lincoln Rockwell, the head of the American Nazi Party, is perhaps a very knowledgable businessman with no political convictions whatsoever. He gets three bucks a head and works the mass rallies of nothing but angry Jews shaking their fists, and wonders why there are so many Jews there. And he probably has two followers who are deaf. They think the swastika is an Aztec symbol.

The Money I'm Stealing

We are living in a degenerate, debauched society, and I am one of the huge cornerstones in the second tower of Babel that we of Satan's growing army are building. Sixty thousand dollars, that's the amount I'll earn next year as a nightclub comedian, and that's probably a conservative figure. A United States Senator earns twenty-two thousand five hundred dollars a year. The average school teacher's pay is seven thousand a year—and I'm sure that's giving rural communities a generous edge. My constructive contribution to society, opposed to, let us say, a senator's or a school teacher's, is another "funny" that dwarfs even the brilliant Chaplin insanities. I'm sure Perry Como feels no guilt pangs about earning more this year than the House of Representatives combined.

You might assume from these writings that I am an extremely moral individual, suffering pangs of conscience in an unjust society, but I am not. I am a hustler like everyone else, and will continue taking the money as long as this mass madness continues. However, I feel that I am a little one up, because I know I am doing wrong and don't stop. You must admit that wrongdoers who are aware of their misanthropy and still persist are a vanishing breed. I have been consciously stealing with no guilt since a child. It seems like only yesterday when Lucky Luciano bounced me on his knee and told me a story of "Little Red Riding Hooker." I've been stealing in the same joyously "legal" manner as some of our illustrious civic leaders, past and present: Jimmy Walker, Huey Long, William O'Dwyer, Big Bill Bonnelie, Sherman Adams.

The above preamble is a roundabout way of explaining to my myriad adverse critics that I am not the "sick, bad taste" comic they accuse me of being. And even if I were, it amazes me that these pillars of society would take time to give me space in their columns when there are so many truly bad taste areas in show business that warrant inspection. The critic who peers over the bedboard of the uneasy marriage of convenience between the advertising department and the editorial room, is really sick. The unhealthy liaison between the advertising department and the bread and butter showbiz columnist results in an ill-conceived pregnancy that cries out for aborting. Without taking you to "that wonderful doctor in Tijuana," and keeping you waiting in the cab, I, Dr. Bruce, will attempt to perform this abortion.

This is an excerpt from an actual interview between myself and a well-known message film producer, whom we shall call Mr. B., due to existing libel laws.

Lenny: Mr. B., actually what is your definition of a message film?

Mr. B.: A film that helps to solve some of society's serious problems. And actually, it is a gamble to produce these films, but we feel if we are helping, then the money shouldn't be a prime consideration.

Lenny: And what do you consider a serious problem?

Mr. B.: Narcotics addiction, and race relations.

Lenny: How do you help the narcotics problem?

Mr. B.: By showing the horrors of the use of drugs.

Lenny: Does a percentage of the profits of the picture go towards rehabilitating addicts, using psychiatric treatment?

Mr. B.: No . . . We show them realism. They are either killed or put in jail, where they belong.

Lenny: When you mentioned improvement of race relations, have you concerned yourself with the fact that Puerto Ricans are extremely discriminated against in New York City? Or that Orientals and Filipinos have difficulty in renting or buying homes in unrestricted areas in California?

Mr. B.: No, there's no market for that. I usually stick to the Negro situation.

Lenny: How do you help in that situation?

Mr. B.: By showing they can live together happily.

Lenny: Do Negroes live next door to you in Malibu?

Mr. B.: No, we have a unwritten agreement among property owners to sell only to Caucasians, otherwise the value of the property would dissipate.

Lenny: Doesn't that sort of defeat the purpose of your film?

Mr. B.: No, you can live together, without living on the same block.

Lenny: I see . . . I understand you have produced several westerns?

Mr. B.: That's true.

Lenny: In one picture, I believe, the hero was a Navajo Indian of a fairly dark complexion.

Mr. B.: Yes, I remember that film.

Lenny: If my memory serves me correctly, there were several rather sensual love scenes, featuring a blue-eyed, extremely Anglo-Saxon type heroine, and the dark-skinned hero, who was very savage and had killed six or seven American cavalrymen.

Mr. B.: Yes . . . What are you building?

Lenny: If the story line called for an American Negro, who was not a savage, perhaps a soldier who fought for the United States in battle, unlike the Indian who killed many American boys, could you then have a scene where the Negro soldier kisses the white girl?

Mr. B.: You could, but it wouldn't be wise. As a producer with integrity, I must protect the stockholders' interests, and a sequence like that would certainly lose our Southern market.

Lenny: I can sympathize with this thinking and actually see some validity in its purpose.

Mr. B.: Then what's your beef?

Lenny: I want the hypocrisy to stop, once and for all. I want all motion picture producers to stop deluding themselves. Profit is the motivation for making motion pictures and justly so. There's never been one motion picture that has dealt with societal problems for the purpose of solving them.

Mr. B.: Very interesting thought.

Lenny: What is the subject matter of your next film?

Mr. B.: It's about the Mafia and their relationship to narcotics traffic.

Lenny: Why don't you do a real shocker and reveal the fact that the Mafia comes from Italy?

Mr. B.: Say, that's an angle . . . Wait a minute, are you trying to be wise?

The Great Hotel Robbery

The following piece originally appeared in *The Realist* and bore a short preface by Editor Paul Krassner:

Recently I spent a week with Lenny Bruce work-vacationing in Wildwood, New Jersey. While driving to Atlantic City in order to indulge in girl-watching on the boardwalk, we would occasionally pass signs stating, "Criminals Must Register."

Said Bruce: "Somebody goes to jail, and after 15 years' incarceration, you make sure you get them back in as soon as you can by shaming anyone who would forgive them, accept them, give them employment—by shaming them on television—'The unions knowingly hired ex-convicts.' Criminals Must Register. In the middle of the hold-up, you go to the County Court House and register. Or does it mean that you once committed a criminal act?"

It is this underlying quality of consistent compassion that gives an added dimension even to Lenny Bruce's occasional excursions —such as the following reaction to a news bulletin—into the world of abstract scatology.

The Great Hotel Robbery

At 12:05 A.M. a cat burglar broke into the fourth floor of the Hotel America in New York City. A suite rents there for $36 a month, and is rented by the year by Wallace Brothers Circus in case a trained bear is pregnant—you know, an animal gets knocked up while working Madison Square Garden.

The Hotel America is the only one that will take a pregnant bear, because the maid only goes in once a year.

Actually, it wasn't a cat burglar, it was a tenant. Somebody in the Flanders Hotel across the street spotted the prowler. "I was looking at the stars through my binoculars," said R. Lendowski, Grand Central Station maintenance porter. "I just happened to be looking and I saw this guy."

When questioned, the suspect said that there was no toilet in his room, that he had recent surgery done on his little toe and walking to the bathroom in the hall was terribly painful, and his roommate caught him pissing in the sink; actually, he didn't catch him, he was just about to start, and he got out of it by saying that he was taking a sponge bath and had to continue bathing from the waist up, while his roommate kept interjecting: "I thought that you were trying to piss in the sink. . . . I once caught a guy doing that in Parris Island. . . . Can you imagine a guy doing that in the sink? . . . The same type of dirty guy that pisses in the ocean. . . ."

So he waited until his friend fell asleep—mumbling about those guys sneak-pissing in the sink.

Then he decided to piss out the window, but felt guilty about it in case some guy that might be a bigger nut on ocean-pissers might be passing by.

What if you pissed on a guy like that?

"Don't move—I see which window that spray is coming from. You! With your hand on the sill, shaking it on the screen!—stop! Okay, you're surrounded, we're behind you. Don't drop anything."

The suspect goes on with his confession:

So I searched out all the possibilities, and I went out on the ledge to make sure I wouldn't get it on anyone. It was 12:05 A.M., and I saw a whole bunch of binoculars from different windows watching me.

Before I knew it, this priest was on the ledge with me. He said, "Son, is this the only way?"

I said, "It's either this or pissing in the sink. The fire engines are here now and I have a choice of confessing as a cat burglar or a peeping tom, but to tell the truth, my roommate won't let me piss in the sink. . . ."

Script for Lenny's Appearance On "The Steve Allen Show"

STEVE ALLEN

And here is is—a young man who, in spite of a frightened society, is skyrocketing to his own orbit.

(STEVE *gestures with hand to opposite entrance.* CUT *to* LENNY FULL FIGURE, *walking slowly to mark.* HE *looks around.*)

LENNY

Here I am, the skyrocket.

(DOLLY IN *fast to tight* WAIST-HIGH SHOT.)

You might be interested in how I became offensive. It started in the fourth grade, when I was depressed and I used to drink a lot. I never was a nasty drunk. But the teacher got bugged with me singing and carrying on, calling Columbus a nut. Smoking, too—I don't know if you can see this tattoo . . .

(*Rolls up sleeve.* CUT *to* LENNY'S *forearm to show the tattoo.*)

I smoked Marlboros when I was six, and grew up. But to leave the ludicrous for a moment, there are many things I find offensive. Nighttime television shows that exploit societal problems under the guise of public service, for instance. Except for one guy on the Coast who does it with a sense of humor—Paul Coates. He found out there are kids sniffing airplane glue to produce some euphoria, to get high on. Back to the day of that exposé.

(CUT *to* FULL FIGURE *until cue.*)

The kid is all alone in his room, and it is Saturday: "Here I am, all alone in the room, and it's Saturday. I'm bored, and I feel the hostility of the adult world. I know what I'll do, I'll make a model airplane. I'll get the balsa wood here, cut out the struts, sand off the wings, and now I'll take a little airplane glue and rub it on the rag here, and I'm—and I'm . . . Ha, ha, it's a *wild* plane. I'm getting loaded! Is this possible—getting loaded on a ten-cent tube of airplane glue? Maybe it's stuffy in here. I'll call my dog over. Flicka, come here and smell this rag, little doggie. Flicka, Flicka, Flicka! I've done it, I've gotten loaded on a tube of airplane glue. I'm the Louis Pasteur of junkiedom."

Now we cut to the toy store—any toy store, perhaps in your town. The kid walks in. Dingalingaling!

(CUT *to tight* HEAD AND SHOULDER SHOT *until cue*.)

"Hello, Mr. Schindler, nice store you got here. Gimme a nickel's worth of pencils, some erasers, and a Big Boy tablet, and *two thousand tubes of airplane glue*."

I was just being facetious when I said that offends me. Words sometimes offend me, like, "Go back where you came from." Motion pictures offend me, the ones that exploit race relations. Hollywood has never made one picture that out-and-out took a stand on integration. A typical "brotherhood" film starts out with Miguel talking to his father.

(CUT *to* FULL FIGURE.)

Miguel is three years old. They are taking the bull away, the bull he raised—the bull he loved. We hear him talking to his father: "Why are you going to take the bull away? I love him."

The father: "Ah, my son, you don't understand."

Miguel: "Don't call me your son. I'm not your son. You're going to kill my bull."

The father: "Oh, if you were only older, you would understand. To kill the bull means three thousand dollars to you in American money."

Miguel: "Kill him!"

Miguel grows up. He is now a young man, nineteen years old. His sister is talking to him over his shoulder as he is looking into the mirror, combing his hair.

(CUT *to tight* WAIST-HIGH SHOT.)

"Miguel, you're going to get into trouble hanging around with the wrong gang. Doctor Mendoza, the shop teacher, says you are making wonderful sandals out of that espresso machine. Are you listening to me, Miguel?"

"Don't bother me. Give me the rubber band for my ponytail."

Dissolve to the exterior of the schoolyard . . .

(*Music.* START MOVING IN *slowly from* FULL FIGURE *to tight* WAIST-HIGH SHOT.)

All the Anglo-Saxon types are bright and shiny, with zipper jackets and switchblade tongues, and Miguel with his poor ripped Madras blazer.

"Listen to me, you guys. One thing I've learned in school. The high school principal put it in my mind, something I can't forget. You know what I learned that I can't forget? I forgot! No, I didn't forget. I am a Spanish guy. Phil is a colored guy. Wong is a Jewish guy, Danny is a Japanese guy. There's a Spanish guy, a colored guy, a Jewish guy, a Japanese guy. My friends, in this country we all have to stick together and beat up the Greeks!"

(Applause cue.)

Then I have another side to my nature. I'm writing a musical with Steve, and it's an interesting story about a married couple who are always fighting, cursing, and yelling at each other. They have two kids, and in seven years, the couple have broken up and gone back together fifty-five times. But they keep going back for the kids' sake.

In the first act, they have recently come back from a marriage counselor, and they decide to stay together—and are together for a whole month without one cross word. And surprisingly enough, they are completely happy, but the kids have gone completely insane. They were so used to the yelling and cursing that the serene atmosphere has made them completely nutty. So, for the kids' sake, they decide to break up.

We find the husband over at his friend's house, complaining.

(STEVE plays the friend.)

STEVE

Hey, Lenny, where's your old lady?

LENNY

Oh, we had a beef. It's all over.

STEVE

Oh? You'll go back together.

LENNY

Naw, that's it. You have a million beefs, and suddenly you realize the final one, and—you won't believe this, but I finally did it. I got rid of her.

STEVE

How did you do that?

LENNY

She left me! But I'm better off. You're better off alone. I'm going to fix up my own pad. I really know how to fix up a pad. I'm going to furnish it little by little. I'll get me some of that shiny black furniture and a bullfight poster, and I'll make one of those coffee tables out of a door, and a satin smoking jacket, and a pearl-white phone, and finally I'll be all alone.

(Song: All alone, all alone,/What a joy to be all alone!/I'm happy, don't you see?/I've convinced you, now how about me?/All alone.)

I don't know what I'm getting so dramatic about. You're better off alone. You can't save a buck if you're married. You wouldn't believe it, but I've had the same dumb suit for the last ten years. You walk into her closet, you can't breathe. I'm going to get a whole bunch of new suits, and an MG and a chick I can hang out with. I'm going to get a chick who likes to drink. I'll have a vodka party. That's it, a chick who likes to drink. But, my wife sure used to look good, standing up against the sink.

Ah, but she's the lowest!
If I saw her, I'd hiss her.
But I guess I do miss her.
I don't want a chick who can quote Kerouac and walk with
    poise,
I just want to hear my old lady say, "Get up and fix the
    bathroom. It's still making noise."

(Song: All alone, all alone./Like a nearsighted dog./Where's the phone?/Ah, but it's better to be/All alone./No more taking out the garbage,/Hear yakking on the phone./I gave her everything,/Even my mother's ring./But to me she was so petty,/Sometimes I wish she was dead./But it would probably take her two hours/To get ready.)

When she's old, she'll be sorry. I can see her, about twenty years from now. "How you doing, Annie? Long time no see. Heard you got married again—four times, huh? Goofed up? Well, that's too bad. Me? No, I always stayed single, invested in property. I just picked up a little place down in Mexico. Maybe you've heard of it, it's called Acapulco. If you're ever down that way, come by and have coffee. Where're you living? Furnished room, huh? Seven dollars a week, with kitchen privileges, with paper drapes. You probably sit in the lobby and watch television. Well, I've got to split now. I just bought Yellowstone National Park. We're going to make a miniature golf course out of it. We'll subdivide, make homes for veterans, you know. . . ."

That's it. Her future spells a murky gloom.
I'll be rich and famous, and she'll
Be living in a furnished room.
But it will be too late;
I won't hear her moan.
I'll be living in my Nob Hill mansion—
Rich, and all alone.

(Song: All alone, all alone,/I'll be rich and all alone.)

Another Sketch for "The Steve Allen Show"

GENE RAYBURN

From four P.M. to six P.M., television viewers are definitely split between watching and listening to profound news analysts or watching the dancing feet of teenage America. At this performance, we find the news too general to satirize, so we have chosen dancing feet.

(DISSOLVE *to* SIX TEENAGE COUPLES *in the foreground, dancing to slow rockabilly tune, with* STEVE *sitting on a raised dais in the background. Rolling credits superimposed:* "ROCK AND ROLL FOR FREEDOM." CAMERA PANS *around the* DANCERS, *who are dressed in typical high school fashion.* ONE COUPLE *is dancing cheek-to-cheek, with the fellow's face facing the* CAMERA, *and as they turn, his* PARTNER *is revealed to be an extremely elderly woman, 65 or 70.* SHE *smiles into the* CAMERA. *We* PAN *from them to* WAIST-HIGH SHOT *of* STEVE *as the music fades.*)

STEVE

We have a lot of nice sides to play and some interesting guests to meet, boys and girls. And I'm pleased to report that they found the one who was slashing my tires. It was an old man, a crank newscaster whose time slot I took, not some innocent teenager as the public would like to believe. Unfortunately, however, he was strung out on dope that some teenager had been selling him.

Before we have our first dance, "The Hot Baby Rock," done by the Switchbladers, we'd like to meet our first guest, Ralph J. Gleason, the most talked-about jazz altoist of the year. Hello, Ralph! Nice to have you aboard.

LENNY

Same to you, sweetie. Like, you crack me up, baby, in front—the way you come on so straight, you know?

STEVE

(Somewhat confused—however, take should be very subtle:) Er, ah, I'm sure a lot of people agree with that philosophy. But to a more definitive analysis of your personality—

LENNY

Hey, baby, don't rank me, now!

STEVE

What?

LENNY

Oh, that's cool, man. I should have known what this scene was going to be, in front.

STEVE

I understand that you are one of the most amazing and brilliant musicians of our time.

LENNY

That's right, baby sweetie. Like, that's the scene that's been goin' down.

STEVE

Do you find that you are criticized by your peers for speaking in the jazz idiom?

LENNY

Who's to say what's normal, baby?

STEVE

Oh!

LENNY

It's just like what Ira Gitler, the great poet, says.

STEVE

What did he say?

LENNY

"Who's to say what's normal?"

STEVE

You're rather young to have the title of "the most amazing musician of our times." How old are you?

LENNY

Twenty-eight years old.

STEVE

How long have you been in the music business?

LENNY

Thirty-five years.

STEVE

Now, wait a minute! You're, er, twenty-eight, and you've been in the music business thirty-five years?

LENNY

That's why they call me amazing.

                            STEVE

Well, you don't seem to me representative of the average
musician.

                            LENNY

I'm *not* a musician, baby. I do record pantomime.

                            STEVE

Where do you get most of your inspiration?

                            LENNY

Wheat germ.

                            STEVE

Oh, you eat wheat germ?

                            LENNY

No, I smoke it.

                            STEVE

Well, thank you, Ralph. And now, let's listen to the Dumbells
sing "Werewolf Mama."

(DISSOLVE *to* LOUIS NYE, TOM POSTON, *and* STEVE'S MOTHER *doing the
tune and the choreography, which I will set. The choreography will be
the high point of the satire. How I will do this: Give me three people to
work with for two days. I will work it out with them, and then* LOUIS,
TOM, *and* S's M *can mimic them, saving wear and tear on the performers. The tune will be pre-recorded, and they will mime it.*)

                    (SONG: "Werewolf Mama")

Well, a man once said, beauty's only skin-deep.

When I look at you, my skin starts to creep.

You're my Werewolf Mama, freaky as you can be.

When it comes to digging monsters,

Frankenstein ain't nothing to me.

Bite me on the neck.

I said, bite me on the neck.

When you stop biting, I'll be a total wreck.

You're my Werewolf Mama, nutty as you can be.

(CAMERA PULLS BACK. *The couples have formed a circle with* DON
KNOTTS *jitterbugging with a real pro jitterbug, who will toss him
around—through the legs, over the shoulder, etc., as a* GUY *wearing a*
LAWRENCE WELK MASK *and smoking a pipe with bubbles coming out of
it walks slowly in front of the* CAMERA *yelling, "Horrible, horrible" in the*
WELK VOICE *that usually screams, "Wonderful, wonderful."*)

NON-MALIGNANT HUMOR: An Impolite Interview

This piece appeared in the February, 1960 issue of *The Realist* and bore the following sidebar/introduction by Editor Paul Krassner:

The first time I saw Lenny Bruce in action was at a rehearsal of *The Steve Allen Show.* I remember that there was a particular punchline which was to be preceded by a drum-roll crescendo ending with a cymbal. The timing was important. They had a run-through "That's good," said Bruce—referring to the drummer—"he feels it."

In much the same way, I think, you will not merely have read his answers in these pages. You will have *felt* them.

The credit goes to Ed Sherman, who—besides being Lenny's "official Boswell"—is the television director of a New York ad agency, writer of the B. Mitchell Reed show on radio station KFWB in Hollywood and under the pen name of George Crater, columnist ("Out Of My Head") for *Down Beat* Magazine.

The interview was conducted in a most unorthodox manner. I submitted some thirty questions—intended only as a loose framework for tangents, digressions, and transgressions—to Sherman, who in turn submitted them to Bruce, who in turn answered them between stints in New York, Minneapolis, Philadelphia, and Miami Beach, returning the answers to Sherman, who in turn translated them.

By "translated" I mean—well, see for yourself. Take the first question, "What's your reaction to the TV quiz scandal?" Lenny first scribbled in pen—*I got a rash.* Superimposed on this, via typewriter, in all capital letters, was the following:

I WANT TO KNOW WHO SANCTIONED THE INVESTIGATION AND HOW MUCH IT COST. I HAVE SPOKEN TO 575 (APPROX FIGURES) AMERICANS THAT WEREN'T HURT AS THE PAPERS SAID. I THINK I WOULD BE SAFE IN SAYING NO ONE CARED. WHEN I SAY NO ONE I MEAN ONLY 25% TOPS.

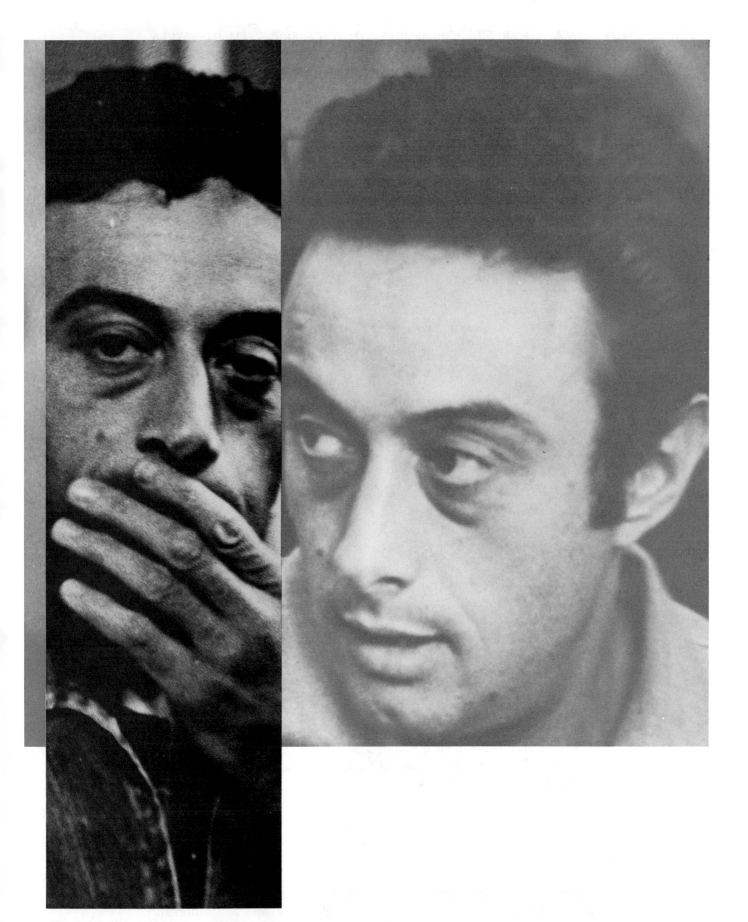

MACK PARKER, POPLARVILLE—THAT DESERVES AN INVESTIGA-
TION, IKE. THEY TOOK HIS POOR BLACK BODY AND DRAGGED HIM
FROM THE CELL. HIS LONELY SHOES, UNDER THE COT IN THE CELL,
TELL THE STORY OF HASTE.

Q. What do you think of the mass-circulation periodicals: *Time*
Magazine? Playboy? McCall's? Others?
A: Others is a reactionary publication.

Q: Last December, Herb Caen had said some nice things about you in his
column. But when May rolled around, *Time* Magazine said that he had
called you "a bore." How come Caen wasn't able to love you in May as
he did in December?

A: Concerning Herb—and I wish you would print this—*Time* Magazine is
a liar! That's pretty strong, isn't it, calling someone a liar? You know what
we think of liars in this country. All those quiz scandal people were liars,
and you know what we thought of them. So if *Time* Magazine is a liar,
they're no better than those other liars—*are* they, boys and girls?

And if the magazine is a liar, doesn't that mean that the people who own
the magazine are liars? That's what *Time* said about those people who
owned those quiz shows—they are bad. Why, who knows—if *Time*,
owned by Luce, lied about this—who knows what *else* they've lied about?
And gosh, if a feller will lie, there's no tellin' *what* he'll do. Gee willikers,
this whole thing is scary.

Oh, I almost forgot—the lie. Herb Caen never said that. *The San Francisco Chronicle* has back issues available, if you want to check.

Q: Would you have done what the other quiz-show contestants did if you
had been in their place?

A: We're all as honest as we can afford to be, with the exception of a few.
Those brave few who never sell out have my admiration and respect. Unfortunately, I'm not with them.

Q: Could you be bribed to do only "safe" material from now on?

A: What's the bribe? Eternal life? A cure for cancer? $45,000,000? What's
the difference what I take—I'd still be selling out.

Q: Joey Bishop—one of the "healthy" comedians—has said that "those
guys (such as Mort Sahl, Jonathan Winters, Shelley Berman, Tom Lehrer
and you) tried their hardest to make it our way; when they couldn't, they
switched." Since this is actually true in your case, what's your reaction?

A: One of hostility towards the chap who wrote the question. Obviously,
you haven't followed my career. Actually, I *continually* switch. Sometimes
I become very philosophical. Other times I'm zany. But certainly I've never
followed "their way." I have always sought to be different.

If you will look in *Variety*, you'll find that the first review I ever got—in
1949—was for a bit I did about Hitler being an M.C. Certainly you
wouldn't call this trite or unimaginative, as opposed to Mr. Bishop, who
has been doing the same thirty minutes of café comedy for the last ten
years. I've done thirty minutes on *The Steve Allen Show* that I'll *never* do
again.

I hope I am better than I was, let's say, five years ago—but that's growing. I hope ten years from now someone makes that same accusation about

me again—"switching," changing, growing. For, as Confucius say: "Anyone who is still doing Confucius jokes, or ever did, will make a good Lodge Commander in the American Legion."

Q: Do you have a favorite joke?

A: No.

Q: George Meredith, in his classic "Essay on Comedy," said that "One excellent test of the civilization of a country . . . I take to be the flourishing of the comic idea and comedy; and the test of true comedy is that it shall awaken thoughtful laughter." How would you apply that to the United States today?

A: I have been all over the world, and this is the best country for a comedian. The most freedom. Do jokes knocking Khrushchev in Russia—are you out of your nut?

Q: Do people misunderstand you and your targets?

A: Continuously!!! Every once in a while, there is a fair appraisal.

Q: As a screenplay-writer in Hollywood, what films did you work on?

A: I've got one single credit—additional dialogue for *The Rocket Man*, starring Anne Francis, Charles Coburn, and Spring Byington. A truly marvelous film achievement, don't you think?

Q: Has anything been happening with you and television?

A: I've turned down one series and just about every show where they wanted me to do a guest spot. TV is a huge kettle boiling on the back of the stove. If you fall in, you're the main course. Boiled out and done—Sid Caesar, George Gobel, Red Buttons, Jackie Gleason, Wally Cox. Who's next to be boiled?

Q: What reactions do you have to the following TV programs: Jack Paar?

A: He seems to have a Corpus Christi image of himself.

Q: The Westerns?

A: You mustn't generalize—*what* Westerns? You must criticize each one individually. For if you damn them all and one was brilliant, you have done a cursed thing.

Q: The teen-age dance parties?

A: Ditto.

Q: Ed Sullivan?

A: I wonder if Julia Meade is really his cousin.

Q: Others?

A: Now, *those* sons-of-bitches should be thrown off the air!

Q: Do you hate anybody?

A: No.

Q: Ralph J. Gleason, a perceptive social critic as well as a brilliant jazz critic, is an ardent admirer of your "colossal irreverence." He has compared your work to that of novelist Nelson Algren, among others. But Algren himself says that people today are bored with ordinary comedy and want to be hurt. Do you think there's any sadism in your comedy?

A: What a horrible thought! If there is any sadism in my work, I hope I— well, if there is, I wish someone would whip me with a large belt that has a big brass buckle.

Q: What would you say is the role of a comedian?

A: A comedian is one who performs words or actions of his own original creation, usually before a group of people in a place of assembly, and these words or actions should cause the people assembled to laugh at a minimum of, on the average, one laugh every 15 seconds—or let's be liberal to escape the hue and cry of the injured and say one laugh every 25 seconds for a period of not less than 45 minutes, and accomplish this feat with consistency 18 out of 20 shows.

Also, he must be able, with little preparation, to do this at least for all people that it is possible to reach. Naturally, this excludes handicapped people such as those who are deaf, blind, illiterate, mentally deficient, etc.

Now understand, I'm discussing comedy here as a craft—not as an aesthetic, altruistic art form. The comedian I'm discussing now is not Christ's jester, Timothy; this comedian gets paid, so his first loyalty is to the club-owner, and he must make money for the owner.

If he can upgrade the moral standards of his community and still get laughs, he is a *fine* craftsman. If he's a chap who needs writers, he is not a comedian, he's an actor—whom I respect also as a craftsman.

Q: What's your capsule opinion of the following persons: Pope John?
A: It's a great title for a Studs Lonigan character.

Q: Billy Graham?
A: It's a great title for a Western TV series.

Q: Bishop Sheen?
A: He bears a great resemblance to the late, great Bela Lugosi. Look closely the next time.

Q: Oral Roberts?
A: Sounds rather lewd.

Q: Brigitte Bardot?
A: It's a great title for a religious TV series.

Q: President Eisenhower?
A: I wonder what he would look like with a toupée.

Q: Nikita Khrushchev?
A: I bet faggots have a ball carrying on with his name.

I just thought of something. I'm sure when the guy wrote these questions he was serious, but at this sitting at the typewriter now I felt just plain silly—and this is a classic example that fuels my argument: you can't classify me, I am somebody different each time out. I'm not bragging about this, but I—Well, it *exists*, that's all I'm telling you.

Q: Were you serious when you said that you want to be a social worker?
A: Probably at the time I said it I was, but unfortunately I am at times irrational and over-emotional, which breeds insincerity.

Q: Gilbert Millstein quoted you in the *New York Times Magazine* as saying: "The kind of comedy I do isn't like going to change the world, but certain areas of society make me unhappy, and satirizing them—aside from being lucrative—provides a release for me. Do you think that this makes you any sort of leech on other people's misfortunes?
A: A good point! Actually, I really am changing a lot of views—but you can't just go around saying that.

Q: By whom have you been influenced in your work?
A: Isn't that an absurd question—I have been influenced by my father telling me that my back would become crooked because of my maniacal desire

to masturbate; by reading "Gloryosky, Zero" in *Annie Rooney*; by listening to Uncle Don and Clifford Brown; by smelling the burnt shell powder at Anzio and Salerno; torching for my ex-wife; giving money to Moondog as he played the upturned pails around the corner from Hanson's at 51st and Broadway; getting hot looking at *Popeye* and *Toots and Casper* and *Chris Crustie* years ago; hearing stories about a pill they can put in the gas tank with water but the "big" companies won't let it out—the same big companies that have the tire that lasts forever; and the Viper's favorite fantasy: "Marijuana could be legal, but the big liquor companies won't let it happen"; Harry James has cancer on his lip; Dinah Shore has a colored baby; Irving Berlin didn't write all those songs, he's got a guy locked in the closet; colored people have a special odor. I am influenced by every second of my waking hour.

Q: Could you sum up, in a single sentence, your philosophy of life?

A: I like Procter & Gamble products because.

On Education and Jack Paar

. . . Okay, some people are born with genetically less intellect than others. But now we go to academic areas of developing intellect. If a kid watches films and TV and cannot identify with education; where it's un-hip to learn or doesn't smack of any virility, then it's sort of a drag.

Now, Jack Paar is a classic case of the mass media. He feels, like a lot of sub-intellects, that the matter with Adlai Stevenson was that he was too much of an intellect. Frig it, Christ was more of an intellect than him, and swung twice as heavy! So intellect doesn't enter into it.

All right, so now Paar's cookin'. Next to him—Hugh Downs, an obsequious, over-solicitous toughie-slicker who's always layin' there dead. He goes, like, "Uh, uh, what is that word, Hugh?"

"That word is non sequitur, Jack."

"Ha, ha! Hugh knows all the big words, boys and girls. He never gets laid, though, ha, ha haaa! Ya see, boys and girls, if ya wanna really shtup the broads, ya gotta be a big honest dunce. Those guys are sneaky who know those big words and a lotta learning, you know?"

And there's the slap in the face for national defense. That's why the Russians orbit the Moon first, because education is the answer for strength, now, okay? If you're looking for that strength, you gotta nurture it along. You can't have Jack Paar, with kids watching him, going like, "Uh, you don't want to get hung up with any big words or any education, man."

WHEN IN DOUBT, LIE LIKE HELL

When the AP interviewed me recently on sick comedy they said, "We know you must really hate someone or something to have your point of view on humor" and I broke into a sweat because, believe it or not, I couldn't think of anybody I really hated.

Interviewer: Boy! Lenny, you hate so many things you can't even make a choice, can you?

Lenny: I hate to shave . . . er . . . I hate *to be alone* . . . I hate . . .

Interviewer: Come off it! What are you trying to prove with that sugar-and-spice crap? Give me some guy that you really hate!

Lenny: Oh . . . a guy! George Bernard Shaw!!

Interviewer: George Bernard Shaw! What the hell you got against him?

(Now first let me tell you—honest to God, you're not going to believe me—but I have never read anything by George Bernard Shaw. I don't know anything about him. I just got that name out of the blue. And besides, he couldn't defend himself . . .)

Lenny: What have I got against him? Did you ever hear about the "Whorton Incident?"

Interviewer: Well . . . er . . . yeah . . . but what the hell, you can't bum-rap someone for . . . Who else do you hate besides Shaw?

(I had him. There wasn't any "Whorton Incident"! I just threw it in. I figured he was too insecure to admit that there was a subject that he wasn't hip to.)

Lenny: Well, do you feel Shaw was right in the "Whorton Incident"?

Interviewer: Lenny, you know better than anyone that you . . . Well, anyway, I have to see something before I believe it.

Lenny: See it? It was in all the papers! His heirs had proof!

Interviewer: Yeah, Lenny, but you know yourself that people are interested in what they can get. . .

Lenny: Getting all you can and sleeping with a guy's wife . . . are two different things! You wouldn't believe it but you can talk to the majority of people and mention the "Whorton Incident" and I mean people that are supposed to be erudite, politically oriented people . . . They look at you like you've given away the secrets of the Rosicrucians.

Interviewer: Lenny, when are you gonna learn that everyone isn't as honest as you?

Lenny: What the hell has honesty got to do with somebody getting a guy's wife started on dope and hanging around lesbians? What was that lesbian's name anyway? They had her picture plastered all over at the time. I forgot her name . . . I think it was Helen. Yeah, that's it, Helen . . .

Interviewer: Yeah . . . Helen! Boy, people are characters . . .

He left, telling me that the story would probably break next week. The following week I looked and looked . . . no AP story! I looked through everything from *The New York Times* to *The Realist.* Then . . . there it was . . . right between Fidel Castro doing one of his TV bits and Elvis sticking a fraulein's bosom in his paratrooper boots in the *New York Inquirer.*

THE PIG THAT WROTE
"PYGMALION"

Lenny Bruce is a comedian who is currently appearing at the "hungry i" in San Francisco. The owner, Enrico Banducci, gave Lenny the go-ahead to expose the famous "Whorton Incident" thrill slaying, dope, and abortion case involving George Bernard Shaw. "He fought the battle with the bottle," said Bruce . . .

George Miller, a friend of mine who is a very big bug on Shaw, called me the next day. "Lenny, you gossip-mongering son-of-a-bitch, you." (It's O.K. to swear in print today since Ginsberg, Kerouac, Ferlinghetti, etc.)

"George, I can explain," I said. "I was talking about Ersatz Shaw, the Venezuelan sculptor. You've seen his work, haven't you?"

George: Yes, of course, but . . .

Stamp Help Out was a concert program that served as a dress rehearsal for *How to Talk Dirty and Influence People*. Rumor has it that following Lenny's arrest for obscenity in San Francisco, he bought back all the copies he'd sold to bookstores around the city, fearing they might be used as evidence against him.

STAMP HELP OUT!

And other short Stories

THE POT SMOKERS

BY LENNY BRUCE

SEE... ACTUAL PHOTOS OF TORTURED MARIJUANAITES

SEE... HOOKERS RESORT TO PROSTITUTION

SEE... SHAME

SEE... SHAME SELL

SEE... SHAME SELL SEA SHELLS AT THE SHIM SHAM!

Dedication

To:

R.S. . . . a V.P. that never gives me any B.S. about my taking so many B's. Ingenious, invincible, indefatigable . . . never asks one to do the impossible 'til he shows you how.

B. . . . Who posed patiently.

H.E.B. . . . Who can make me laugh and cry and get horny quicker than anyone I know.

D.R. . . . My friend, who took the cover photo . . . always maintains an inexplicably cool attitude and is always in control . . . EXCEPT ONCE.

F.L. . . . My secretary . . . "Behind those glasses there's a lotta woman" . . . who had faith in my ability and understood my lack of finances. What she did after work is her business. She took dictation at any time, any place, wherever I was, whoever I was with, and never asked to join in . . . and never told Alex Freeman of The Inquirer . . . but did slip a few notes to Charles McHarry of the New York Daily News and Arthur Gelb of The New York Times.

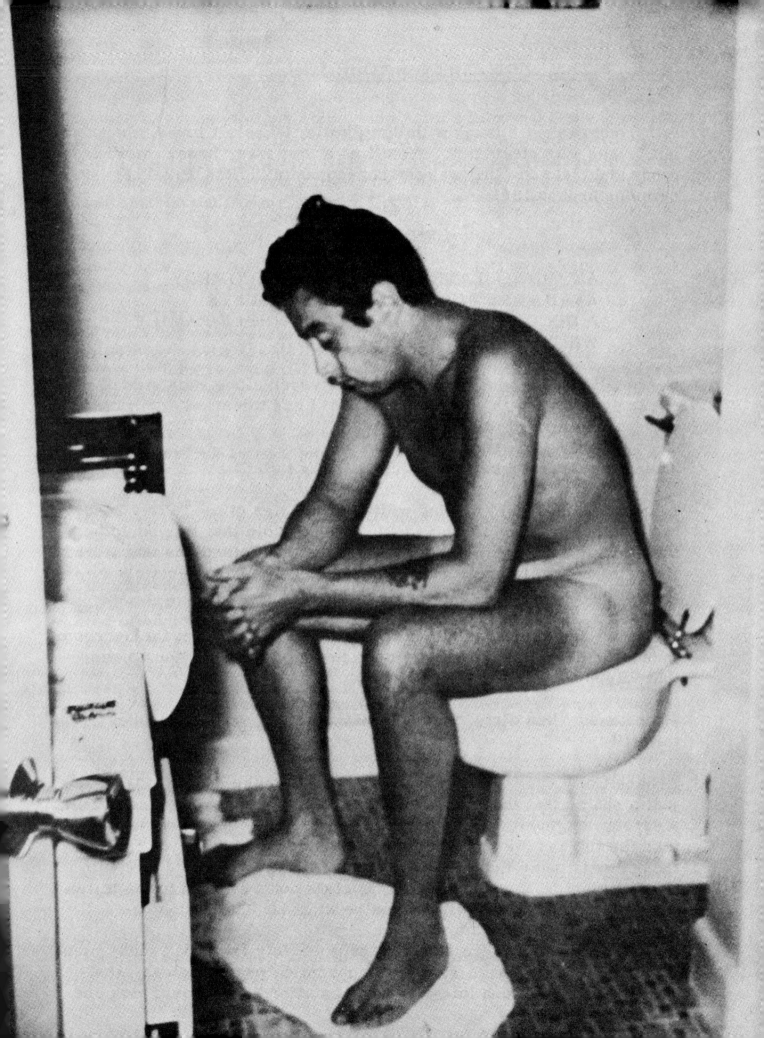

A CHIPPIE OFF THE OLD BLOCK

It was Meatless Tuesday, and American women glutted themselves with the tales of the lewd, immoral European women who were giving up trim for chocolate bars and cigarettes. Our women, because of their Victorian standards, had a far superior moral code. One of the reasons, perhaps, was that Hershey is in Pennsylvania and American Tobacco is in North Carolina; because they sure gave up a lot of nooky for nylons. The housewives of the oil-rich Middle-East countries, where promiscuity is negligible because of the culture, must have been amazed at the European hershey hookers and the American chicks who would give up pussy for some petrol.

1943 was my first taste of being treated as an adult. It was to a small degree. In Boot Camp, you were treated as an Eagle Scout. I couldn't understand the dread and sickening anticipation that the married guys felt. Guys that had been married from six to eight years and had a couple of kids--they were leaving, leaving to go overseas, leaving their homes, their children, and their wives; leaving their sweet wives all alone. The wives would have to be brave to endure maybe three, four years of maddening desperation, looking at that calendar: "Was my period on the sixth or the seventh?"

The thing that delighted me was that half of the erring wives were involved with the guy's brother, a Marine who was in on leave from Iwo Jima. "My own brother! What could he have been thinking?"

What could he have been thinking? He could have been thinking that his brother's wife was a beautiful woman, with long soft brown hair that never smells from cigarettes. His own brother! Who else? They were raised in the same environment; chances are that their tastes are quite alike. The after-statement of "Dear John" reading that used

to flip me was, "Christ, her own brother!" I couldn't imagine how those things could have been worked out.

The kind of woman who never uses a razor on her legs or underarms and never uses talc; the kind of woman that is never obvious: she can wear a loose cotton housedress . . . but yet has the good life-scent of the white dove, and a body underneath that does up doctors who have probed, cut, sewn, and rubber-glove-fucked so many women that it has become a task.

"Mm, your adenoids seem quite normal; perhaps the trouble is respiratory. Unbutton your blouse a moment, and we'll listen to the old ticker. There's quite a bit of flu going around, and I . . . there uh . . . actually . . . ah, ah . . . here, ah . . . Oh God, oh merciful Mother of God, what a body! You're so tan and yet so white. Please may I touch you? Not as a doctor . . . Let me unbutton my shirt and feel you close to me. Please don't push me away. Here, let me . . . please . . . Oh God, I'm losing my mind; let me latch the door; let me just kiss it, that's all I want to--Oh please please please please. Please just touch it, just--look at it. I do respect you. I just can't catch my Goddamn breath."

A doctor, besides having spent fourteen years involved with the academic and practical aspects of medicine; a doctor who has been exposed to the sensual verbalizing of Browning and Flaubert, and to the colors of Renoir; is reduced to the common denominator by that certain kind of woman and finds himself using the blank verse of grammar-school cafeterias: "Whew, you're really built!" That certain kind of woman; or is it that that doctor is the same with every kind of woman; or is it that for every woman--or maybe an extension on the aphorism that for every man, there's a woman . . . the kind of woman that is hornier than her hollywood screen portrayer with her wide-screen titties.

Angela was 28 when I met her. Her father and mother had just died, and she and her brother inherited the business: a 13-by-15-foot Italian-American grocery store and soda fountain with living quarters in the back that she shared with her brother, who went to CCNY at night. He took care of the combination grocery-store-and-soda-fountain during the day, and she worked there at night.

Whenever you hear of the indiscreet sexual activities of a stepfather who is arrested for molesting his wife's fifteen-year-old daughter, you can be sure there's an Angela involved; the kind of chick that makes an elevator operator feel that he possessed great powers of control because he went eighteen floors and didn't rip off her dress.

I walked into the store in white hat and dress blue uniform, announced by the little tin bell, the "candy store burglar alarm." The phrase "Someone's in the store" is filled with innuendo; it means, "Go in the front and see they don't steal anything."

I was truly a man of the world—a fighting Navy man, 127 pounds of steel, an unshaven face, and a broken-out forehead. I knew my way around. My Endicott-Johnson shoes, still new and stiff, kept me slipping around like Joan Davis doing an eccentric dance number. With eight dollars hid in my shoe and a dollar in my hand, I walked up to the counter and spoke out softly, but yet with a jaded-enough tone so that she would know I'd been around; that all these joints were alike to me—one night the Ritz; the next night, Mamie's place in Shanghai:

"Pepsi, please, and a nickel bag of potato chips."

She ripped the stapled chips away from the cardboard and studied my face and looked at me for at least a minute. When she finally spoke, her words stunned me. I would never expect a woman who looked like that to talk that way to a bon vivant such as I:

"How the hell did you get gum in your hair?"

"The guy that sleeps in the bunk above me stuck it on the edge of my rack. I thought I got most of it out."

"C'mere. I've got some benzene, it'll take it out."

I followed her through the blue rayon portals that separated the industry she was president of from her home. I sat on a soda box and watched her rumble through the "medicine cabinet," a cardboard box under her bed. She soaked the rag and stood over me, gently kneading the by-product of the rubber tree from my hair.

As her weightless thigh pressed against my cheek, I felt a strange pleasant ambivalence. The gum was long gone, and the store bell had tinkled and bonged and clarilloned 'til it was hoarse—a guardian bell with a disinterested ward.

We kissed, touched, and related in voiceless tones sounds that inhabit the aura and time of first love. I wonder if that Indonesian rubber tree worker ever dreamt of the delicious fruit that I received from his labor.

Her brother Guido was scuffling through college, working days in the store and a part-time machine shop gig at night, leaving the store unprotected and Angela gloriously uninhibited.

My first love was nurtured in a setting of Medaglia D'Oro café, Ace combs, and Progresso tomato puree. Guido, Angela's brother, would join us for coffee after his nightly involvement with school. He had clawed his way through two years of college with a child-support case and a debt-ridden grocery store, a father and mother who both suffered and finally passed away from pleurisy.

I didn't realize it at the time, but the entrance I made upon Angela's life was ill-timed. She had neglected the store. The registered letter from the Appellate Court, Judge Morris L. Bromberg, handed down the decision that they had to forfeit the store and its possessions so that they could be sold in order for the exploited landlord to receive a portion of the thirteen months' back rent.

Guido reread the letter and then the envelope and then looked at his school books and started crying. Not the kind of crying you see on the stage; there is no sound or movement with the tears.

"Angela, you better move in with Frances and Maria and help them with the bakery, and I'll—"

He had it figured out: he could have

finished school for a little over $1,800, but it was all over now. He left dragging his right foot, a black shiny cumbersome nine-inch-sole corrective shoe; he ran hopping out of the door into the sweat-laden breeze of New York in August--

Several days later, as I left for overseas, I wondered if I were ever to see Angela again, or if her brother would ever get a chance to go to school.

Years later, while working in Boston, Guido came backstage to see me. As I glanced at the college ring on his left hand, he smiled. Before I could ask him about college and Angela, he said, "After I read that letter from Judge Bromberg, I was down in the dumps. I had about $180. About a week later, it was Angela's birthday. I invited her up to this little apartment I had; it was one of those kitchen-apartment hotel rooms. I bought a cake for her. We had a nice meal, and when she went home, I felt so alone and got so depressed that I got the bottle of the sleeping pills that the doctor gave me when my foot kept me up and swallowed about twenty of them. I sat there waiting to die, and it seemed hours and nothing was happening.

In fact, I was starting to feel good, so I turned all the gas jets on. I guess it was about fifteen minutes later and those pills really had me loaded, and I forgot where the hell I was and what the hell I was doing, and I took out a cigarette and started to light it and blew myself and a cranky night worker, who was always bitching that the desk never gave him a wakeup call, out the side of the building.

"He was killed instantly, and I was in the hospital for three and a half months. Some smart lawyer read about it and visited me, and I signed a paper, and he sued the owner of the building for negligence and collected $12,000. I gave Angela two grand, and she went to Puerto Rico for a vacation. She married some Arthur Murray instructor she met down there. It's funny, I never figured Angela to settle down, much less marry a teacher."

Married: that meant she would be kissing someone the same way she kissed me. How could she call anybody else Daddy? Would she take gum out of his hair the same way she did mine? Frig Wrigley!

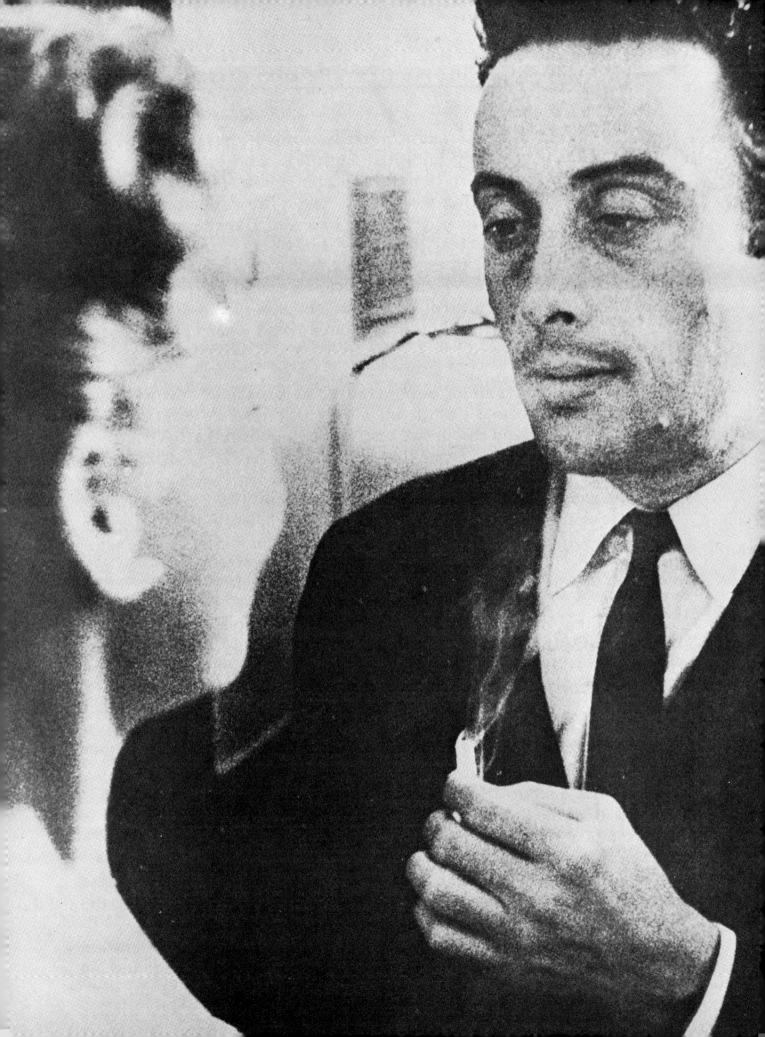

HOW DIRTY IS YOUR TOILET ?

"Anybody can get a laugh with dirty 'toilet jokes'; it takes talent to get laughs with clean stuff. You'll go a long way, Lenny; you're funny and clean." That was the consensus of Show Biz V.P.s' opinions around 1951.

Lenny Bruce
An Immaculate Conception of Comedy
Available for Weddings, Banquets
A Good, Clean Show for the Whole Family
Write--Wire--Phone 555-7543

Tears filtered through my lashes and rivered along each side of my nose, overcome with emotion, blessed: I had talent. I didn't have to resort to dirty toilet jokes.

Then I started thinking . . . How dirty is my toilet?

I lay in bed that night, tossing with my fantasies of the "dirty, resort-to-anything-for-a-laugh" comedian. It's feasible that this could be the start of making the word "resort" dirty. Comedians who work resorts, entertaining people that go to resorts, are certainly Resorting.

I couldn't control my religious fervor. I exploded from the bedroom, thundered down the hall, threw open the door to that odious place, that "Resort."

I screamed, "You dirty, filthy, stinky, crappy, Commie, dopey toilet! Thank God I don't have to Resort to you to make people laugh. It's just a shame that there aren't laws to keep you and your kind out of a decent community. Why don't you go back where you came from . . . take the tub and the sink and that jellyfish hamper with you? Even though their name isn't as dirty as yours, anybody who'd live with a toilet must be Resortaddicted. Purists don't even go to the toilet. All I can say is . . . it's lucky you're white!!"

If I felt that toilets were a detriment to society, I wouldn't make mention of it unless there was need--economic, psychological, whatever. I have as much integrity as I can afford. If I could pick one word to strike from the dictionary, it would be the adverb "never." I love my country, would give allegiance to no other, nor would I choose any other for my home. And yet if I followed Powers or perhaps three other men from the U.S. Service and saw them lying bound and nude with their insurgents pouring white-hot lead into a funnel that was inserted in their mouth, they wouldn't even have to heat another pot for me. I would give them every top secret, make shoe-shine rags out of the flag, denounce the Constitution, and give them the right to kill every person that was kind and dear to me. That's how low I am, that's what I would resort to to keep from getting a molten lead gargle. I spent four years in the Mediterranean and saw starving priests, doctors, and judges. It's amazing how ethics erode when the recession builds.

After the theaters started closing and the nightclubs felt the absence of war, some showpeople couldn't get work and actually did have to resort to toilets--not discussing them, but cleaning them. The first performers to feel it were the magic acts. That was the agents' postwar cry: "If I had a job, don't you think I'd be glad to give it to ya? They're just not buying dance teams anymore. They're not buying magic acts anymore." The only place you could get a club date was at some broken-down Kiwanis hall, and they were getting scarce.

What happens to people whose vocation becomes outmoded? Elevator operators who were replaced by buttons; no place to go. What kind of a guy would want to be an elevator operator anyway? Except some guy who wants to return to a womb with a door he can open and close at different floors.

Arnold and Rona were a dance team, a by-product of World War II. Not a very good dance team; everything good was to be sent overseas to be killed.

The people at home lived in a constant state of ambivalence, guilty but glad. Glad that they weren't a bunk-buddy of the G.I. who was enjoying that final "no wake-up call" sleep on his blood-puddled mud mattress.

It would be rather interesting to hear his comment if we could grab a handful of his hair, dragging his head out of the dirt, and ask his opinion on the question that is posed every couple of decades. The contemporary shouts, "How long are we going to put up with Cuba's nonsense?" or "Just how many insults can we take from Russia?"

I was at Anzio. I can take a lot of insults. I would rather have mud thrown in my face than have a Mauser throw my face into the mud. If you're of the Do-it-to-them-before-they-do-it-to-you school, you go ahead; and I'll buy the bonds and sing the "We Did It Before, and We Can Do It Again" war song. As a Northerner, I have hummed the tunes that described the decadent injustices of all I have warred with, from the one agent who nurtured me, gave me my first big break, but collected commissions on jobs I got myself. "Taxation Without Representation"--that agent was England.

After we resolved our conflict with the villainous English, the next were the Indians, who had some absurd philosophy that since they were here before us, they had some claim upon the land. Setting the antecedent to Nazi purging, we proved to those dunderheads the correctness in the Aristotelian aphorism, "Possession is nine-tenths of the law." If you have any doubts, if you're ever in Miami, drive to the one-tenth: the Seminole Indian Reservation, the mosquito-ridden, agriculture-resistant Everglade swamps.

The next suffering people we had to liberate were the Mexicans. We took Texas and California but, always maintaining a concept of justice, left them a land where holy men could walk: the desert.

Then the war that bore the dubious title of "Civil" and, continuing our hollow rodomontade behavior, we involved ourselves in

the War to End All Wars. After going out on a limb, other wars followed, especially the one that took courageous Americans, heroic Russians, invincible Englishmen, and the indefatigable French to win. Sharing moral unity and having God and Irving Berlin on their side, they censured those who offended the principles of Christianity: the Italians. The Pope, possessing the clairvoyance of a deity, did not flee to Argentina, thereby escaping an Eichmann fate.

I am not offended by wars as I am not offended by rain. In my opinion, they are both motivated by greed. War--direct result of "I ain't got; you got. You gimmee . . . You say you ain't got enough to gimmee? O.k., I'm civilized, I accept that . . . I'll accept that 'til I'm empty. Now not only I ain't got, but I _need_! So I'm takin'!"

The Korean War weeded out some of the population and helped the housing problem, but didn't leave the dramatic impact that World War II did. As the impact lessened, so did the desire to escape lessen; and all the escape hatches--the bars, nightclubs, and theaters--felt it. Of course, all the people who related economically to these media felt it.

Arnold and Rona, the dance team I was discussing before the word "war" set me off on that digression paragraphs ago, were part of the milieu. Arnold handled the business, making the rounds to the agents. Arnold, with his eyebrow pencil mustache, fighting for breath in the abundance of the icy wind that trilled and wheezed around in the Brill Building, echoing with the sound of a behemoth Goliath with bronchitis. Bored with building-jousting, the wind sought a more mobile target.

"Arnold and Rona." They shared equal billing, except for the chapped thighs that Arnold received in the February weather. Arnold and Rona met years ago at the Arcadia Ballroom, "dancing nitely, fun for all ages, no minors allowed." Rona had been fortunate: she had a classical ballet background received at the Borough Hall Y.W.C.A. every Tuesday between 8:00 and 9:00. (That's if the Public Speaking Salesmanship Class convened on time.) She had a big keester and no nay-nays. She was built like a pear: ballet helped her, so she didn't have any fat--very muscular; a muscular pear. A muscular pear with platform shoes from Kitty Kelly's, net stockings that had been sewn so many times they looked like varicose veins, and black satin Ruby Keeler tights. The crotch not exactly split, but giving. A top that was solid sequinned, which the dry cleaner hated. She loved this top; a tap dancer sold it to her when she and Arnold were playing the State Theatre in Baltimore. She said she wasn't going to use it anymore because Henry Lee Tang was going to set a new number for her with college sweaters and megaphones and stuff, so she got it at a steal for $8.00. The hoofer had bought it from a drag queen they worked with at the Greenwich Village Inn when they had straight acts. They had female impersonators, and then the straight acts would work in between. The drag queen said he paid $12.00 at Maraham's for the sequins alone. At $8.00 it was cheap, and it sure was pretty. But it flattened out her bust and was too big in the shoulders.

Arnold lived for flamenco and spent all of his time in the rehearsal halls striking a familiar flamenco pose. The way he stood looked to Rona as if he were applauding his own ass. Arnold was a faggot, an out-and-out flaming faggot. He didn't swish, but he was much Marge, sort of like an old auntie. He was so obvious that everyone knew that he was a faggot except Rona, his partner, and her family. They didn't know because they were very religious, and Arnold acted just like a lot of ministers that she had seen in her formative years.

Arnold chose show business because it was best for him since he was so obviously Nellie; not that show people have more of a Christian attitude toward their fellow men and are less likely to look askance at one who is out of step. It's just that their ego is so big, and they are so self-centered that they haven't the time to concern themselves with the individual and his problems.

Like drug addicts, Arnold's homosexual traits were environmental. He wasn't "born that way." He was once introduced to a group that gave him identity; he was a busboy at Gimbel's, and after one summer at Atlantic City, he came back a faggot. He could just as easily have come back a junkie or a water-skier or a Jehovah's Witness, but he came

back as <u>something</u>. "At least I'm something-- I belong to a group. I share their notoriety, their problems, their laughter." In a crowded arena, the cliché "It takes one to know one" is quite a profound philosophy.

Arnold blossomed in this anthropopha-gistic society. He became poetic in his facility to relate in the argot of the citi-zens of Gropery and the country of Padded Basketdom; the esoteric delight in passing a complete stranger and shrilling, "Get you, Annie!"; the same idiomatic rapport of the nighttime junkie who is looking to score. Arnold became a faggot because he wanted to belong.

Arnold and Rona met in a tryout for the Harvest Moon Ball at the R.K.O Albee in Brooklyn. I was number two on the vaudeville bill that accompanied the tryouts.

In between the big dates, there were many theaters in the New York area that had vaudeville for one night. You got $17.50 for a single, and a two-person act got about $25.00. All the acts were working these dates just for a showing; the money was secondary because that's when the rent was due, on the second.

VODVIL, EVERY FRI. SAT. SUN.

BINGO EVERY TUES.

Free Dish to Ladies

R.K.O. Jefferson, Fourteenth Street
Rehearsal 7:30 P.M.

When I got off the crosstown shuttle and cranked out a penny's worth of semi-faded chocolate-brown nuts, I always wondered how the hell those nuts got faded in the vending machine down in the dark subway. Maybe they were nickel nuts that didn't sell in Miami because of a short season, and they went there next. But they always tasted good. I don't know the ingredients of the chocolate, but I assume they were certainly superior to M&M's. They wouldn't melt even in your mouth. The one on 42nd Street near Hubert's Museum was the best. It was integrated with engage-ment rings, wee harmonicas, and teeny red dice.

I washed down the peanuts with a Nedick's hot dog from the orange drink stand next to the theater. "Clark Gable, Spencer Tracy, 'Boom Town.' Rough, Raw, Ripping: Men with Hearts of Iron and Fists of Steel."

The rehearsals were quite different than most writers portray. The movie is on, and you have just a talk-over rehearsal with the five guys in their room, which is behind the pit or sometimes in back of the screen. The backstage manager isn't a kindly old man called Pop; he's a cranky motherfucker who keeps yelling, "How many times am I going to tell you assholes there's no smoking back here?"

Count Marco and Company, a brother and sister high-wire act, were really bitching at the outdoor agent. They had never worked in the States. He had seen them at the Wallace Brothers' Circus while they were touring in Canada and he was selling stocks in between bookings. He talked them into coming to New York with the promise of getting them on The Ed Sullivan Show or a date at the Latin Quarter. They explained to him they had never worked in any nightclubs, since their act required a fifteen-foot ceiling clearance after their rig was up. Actually, it needed about fifty-three feet for their rig and act.

For $25.00, the Count had them sweating out seven hours of rig assembly, reworking the antiquated floor plates that existed in the theater, completely severing the tip of his forefinger and badly bruising his knee with a miscalculated hammer and being fed up with Arnold playing Florence Nightingale with his cold compresses and shrieking, "You're so strong!"

With no cooperation from an unsympathetic theater manager who played fifteen different acts a week, the Count finished hopelessly, stripping a lug-nut thread on the second guidewire when he heard the backstage manager: "What the hell do you people think this is, a Goddamn rehearsal hall? You better make sure you clean up every bit of that crap after you're finished." The Count kissed his bruised forefinger, chucked Arnold in the ass, walked over to the water cooler, picked up the stage manager, and threw him directly through the center of the screen, a moment after Spencer Tracy had walloped Clark Gable on the chops, knocking him down. I didn't know if the audience thought it was Clark Gable getting up. As I think back, I wonder

if some guy saw him flying out and envisioned the commercial aspects and formulated the idea for Cinerama.

They took the Count to the 36th Precinct, leaving his sister alone with the grim prospect of doing a nine-minute act with no partner. The thing that really cracked me up was the expression on her face when she looked up and saw the rig. From the top of the bar, there was only three feet to the ceiling.

I crouched on my haunches in the wings, and they introduced the double. I waited to see what the hell she was going to do as a single, with not enough room to recline, much less stand. Believe it or not, she went out and did eight minutes; she chinned herself 571 times.

Some Daily News people were there, since they were sponsoring the Harvest Moon Ball affair, and Maria Montez and Sabu were supposed to crown the king and queen. They didn't show up, so R.K.O. sent a new western star they were grooming. He got picked up on a drunk driving charge, so it ended up with an usher giving out the awards.

Rona and Arnold never got a chance to go on, and it was really a shame because Arnold had spent the whole day up till show time making darts in the sequin top. It looked pretty good: at least the shoulders fit, but it made her look a little hunchbacked.

The outdoor agent stood backstage, mute, staring at the hole in the screen. When outdoor acts get temperamental, it really manifests itself visually. he was a bitter man on the low rung of the marquee-bulb ladder. His clients were mostly circus performers. He got bugged with the guys who stood outside the Strand Building: "how's Frank Buck?" "Hey, Phil, how much will it cost me to get two elephants for the American Legion stag we're having?" Phil wanted to belong also and, being a man who is concerned with carnal lust, he knew nightclub agents had a good wedge as far as getting laid. with aerial acts, even if there is any good-looking broad that he had a chance to book, she always had hair under her arms and was extremely earthy and always had a bush instead of hair.

So when he saw Arnold and Rona, he didn't see a dance team, he saw a wedge. I introduced him to Kona, and as a reward, was invited to partake in the 85¢ (if it's a family dinner for three) dinner at Chin Lee's Chinese cuisine and show. A Chinese restaurant with a floor show is as incongruous as a house of God with gambling. But Chin Lee's had its showgirls, and the Church has its Bingo. Now if they could only get together, drunks could find a Chinese restaurant that was open at seven in the morning.

THE BUST

A Catholic priest was excommunicated last week in Syracuse, New York. The offense was rather unusual. The incriminating testimony was bizarre.

The witness for the Papal State testified, "I'm an ex-Marine from Bay Parkway in Brooklyn. When I moved up to Syracuse, I joined the Sacred Heart Order and went to Confession.

"I began to get suspicious when the priest kept telling me to confess the same story over again: the one about the mother, the daughter, and her oddball brother on Fire Island: 'Tell me again the part about how you ripped her dress, and the mother screaming, "Me next, big boy!" '

"Seein' as how he enjoyed the stories so much, I just started making up new ones, and it just got wilder and wilder. Then he started inviting friends in to hear the stories, and there it was--High Mass; I was up there, telling these far-out stories to 2,000 people. They didn't have anything to do with the Bible; they were just good old horny stories. Some-times, if the crowd would get really whipped up, I'd throw in a few craphouse poems like 'There Was An Old Man From Nantucket.' Father Martin really got his gun off on that one, and people were going to church every night, bringing cake and wine. It was a real party!

"One Tuesday night, I was really hung over and I had a couple of my asshole buddies there that I wuz on Omaha Beach with. They had a fifth, and we started beltin', and I introduced them to Father Martin. They con-fessed some stories that really got him crazy. Leroy--he's from Raleigh, North Carolina--told him that one about the rich fag he beat up at three o'clock in the morning on Fisherman's Wharf in San Francisco, and how the old fruit kept yellin', 'Don't stop even if I tell you to.' Father Martin got in a damn giggling fit, and when everyone was seated, we started off the service with that song, 'Ta Ra Ra Boom Te Ay, Did You Get Yours Today?' and then right into a medley of 'Mr. Wong's Got the Biggest Tong in Chinatown.' And that's when we got raided. . . . "

THE POT-SMOKERS

The following is a pictorial and written
thesis on the dread narcotic, <u>Cannabis</u> <u>sativa</u>; also known--in the idiom of those poor
souls who are involved with this living
death--as pot, grass, mota, yelba, or the
very clandestine "my friend," or "anything"
over the 'phone to avoid detection: "Did
your friend get in yet?" or "Did he bring
anything?" or the vulgarity, "Is anything
happening?"

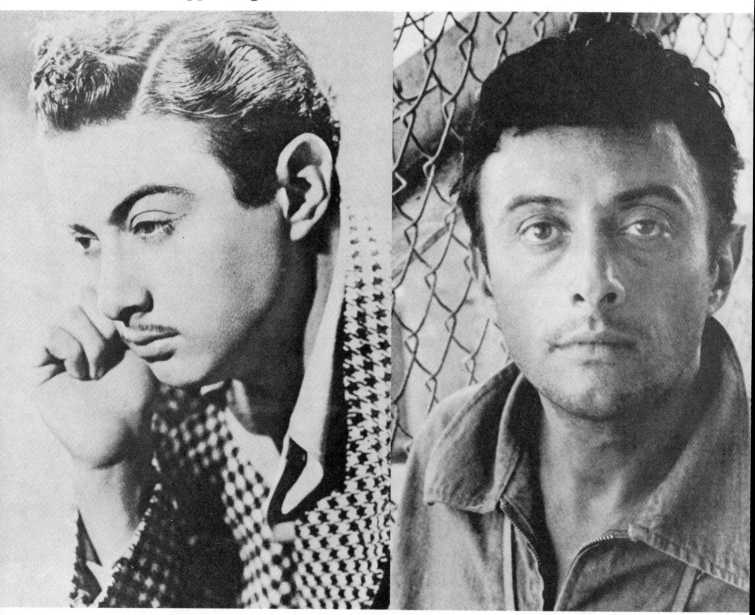

Russell Dreck, Before   Russell Dreck, After

Russell just tried it once, on a dare. "The man came around the schoolyard"--an extremely esoteric bit of information, because the real big pushers have spread around the fable, "Just ask any jazz musician." Schoolyards are the place where most of the marijuana is sold. In fact, a stranger can go into any town, into any schoolyard during recess; and when the teacher says, "Do you want milk?" you reply, "No." And then the man comes up and gives you a free marijuana. That's why you see the whole classroom with the children's heads on their desks, napping (idiom in the underworld: nodding).

Russell's mother knew there was something wrong with Russell. She and the seventeen-year-old had, up to now, been inseparable. His indifference was a cold stab to his poor mother's heart but a relief to his father, who was damn lonesome.

One night, Russell wasn't listening to The Answer Man with his mother, as they had done for years. Mrs. Dreck looked over at her husband, who was viciously breaking the foremast inside of Russell's ship-in-the-bottle. "I wonder where Russell is. It's time for The Answer Man; he'll be on in a minute," Mrs. Dreck said bravely, biting back the tears.

"Why don't you ask him? He knows all the goddamn answers."

What happened to Russell?

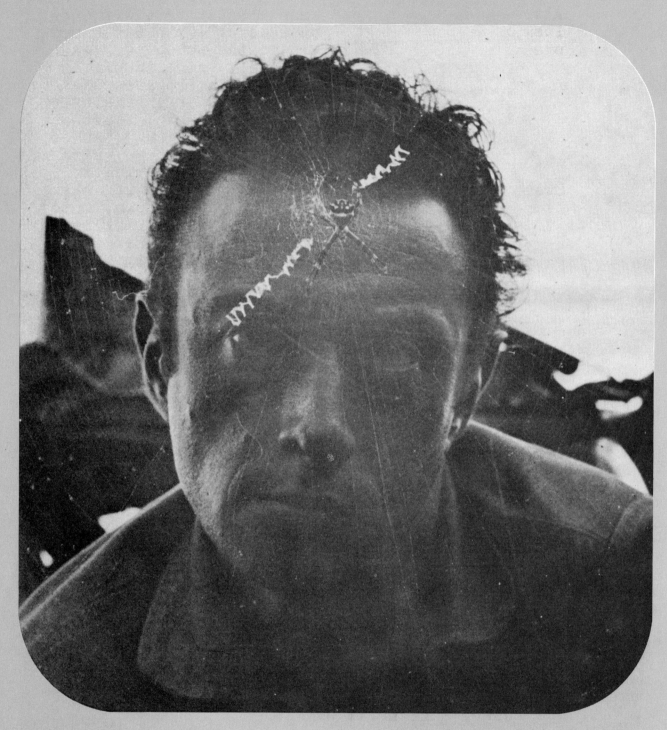

Russell Dreck sat in his room in a hypnotic trance, un-
aware that the cobwebs in the plant his mother had
given him for Easter had gotten out of hand. He sat
there dejected, listless, pepless, and—the most tragic of all to a warped mind—potless. He hadn't
touched his baton for a week. His boots and tassels
lay in the corner, unused. Hmmm, he's wearing those
sandals again that the beatnik gave him.

Russell's mother decided to call her older son, Steve.

Although he was not as sensitive as Russell, he was
lucky: he loved the outdoors and could never fall
prey to the tomblike existence that befell his brother. Steve loved the open country. His mother called
him up in Oregon, where he was selling shingles and
siding. He not only liked to live outside, but he
liked to sell things that fit on the outside. (Some
narrow-minded authorities had put some of his friends
on the inside, but that's another book.)

Steve listened to his mother's impassioned tale of the
bearded beatnik and his brother's grapple with Satan.
Steve went out to avenge his brother. Steve was arrested several months later by local authorities, upon the insistence of the B'nai B'rith, after breaking
the jaws of two Rabbis whom
he mistook for beatniks.
He discovered this too
late when, instead of
spouting Kerouac, they
screamed "Givalt!"

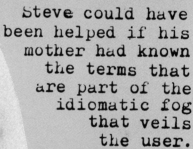

Steve could have
been helped if his
mother had known
the terms that
are part of the
idiomatic fog
that veils
the user.

JOINTS- IDIOM FOR MARIJUANA CIGARETTES

Derivation: Many ingenious hiding places where pushers conceal their narcotics-- knee joints, elbow joints. This term and place of concealment was exposed by a Royal Canadian Mountie who offered to Indian-wrestle one of the pushers who was under surveillance and who, during the contest, was unable to keep his elbows down. They kept flying toward the ceiling.

Author shown holding a part of a marijuana cigarette.

A JOINT

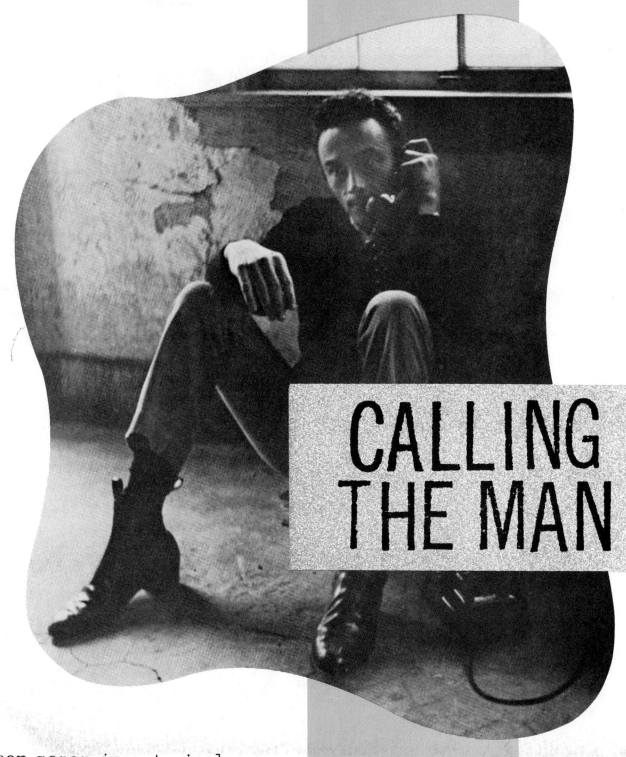

CALLING THE MAN

Author poses in a typical
marijuana user's apartment.
The couple who lived here have
been taken into custody. The
desperation of the couple is
shown by the absence of the
wall-to-wall carpeting, which
they smoked at the end. "Calling the man" frustrates the
user when the cliché, "If a
man answers, hang up" is used.

PUSHER

Not to be confused with the Bronx secretary rejection, "Don't get pushy."

THE CONNECTION

Posing in front
of a marawanny
bush is the con-
nection--a para-
site that thrives
on the tragic
despair of a
seamy world; from
which the under-
world term, "If
you see me with
the man, cool it,"
was derived.

A GOOD COUNT

Sometimes, to boost business, the connection will give the user a little extra. Here is the author with (in the background) an ounce that he is protecting.

A SHORT COUNT

If the user is of noble blood, marijuana has been known to reduce the individual's physical size. Count Berazzo and Count Putzolob are pictured.

MANICURING

The process used in separating the tobacco from the twigs. The author is pictured here with a confiscated manicuring machine.

HOLDING

User's term, relative to possession of the drug. Here is the author showing "The Holding Method."

Marijuana that is not smoked. The user sits approximately eighteen inches from the stalk and inhales the fumes.

ZONKED

THE VIPER

A rare snake that can be smoked. Not to be confused with smoked lox or ham.

WATER PIPE

Addicts interviewed reported that the water pipe gives pleasurable effects. However, they have difficulty in keeping it lit, which brings despair. This method is the derivation of the phrase, "He's a cool guy."

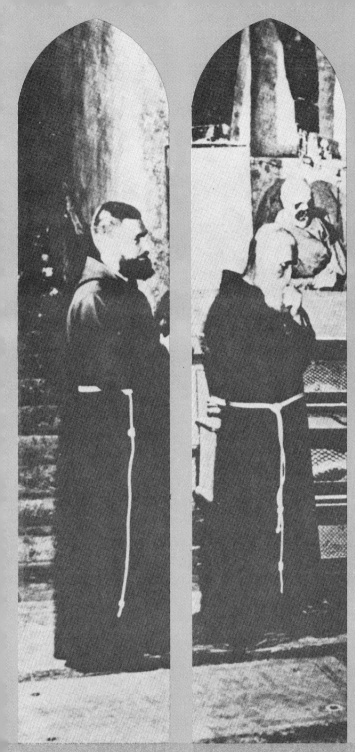

LAYING UP

After the drug has been smoked, the addict goes into a state of suspended animation. Laying up is not to be confused with nodding. Of the two standing men pictured, which one is nodding? Which one is about to nod?*

*Test question from "How to Tell If Everybody Did Up Before You Got There."

EUPHORIA

Games played af-
ter narcotics
take effect.

"Are you going to cop tonight?"
After smoking hemp, the cos-
tume fetish seems to manifest
itself.

COPPING

EUPHORIA COSTUMEA

A usually normal
middle-aged busi-
nessman trapped in
Euphoria costumea.

A HEAD

After smoking the weed, the users sometimes involve them- selves in a macabre game called "doing up the car." The indi- vidual's head is usually the only part left. Special Agent Harold Horney poses.

KNOCKERS
KNOCKERS

Hermaphrodite narcotics-
users who have a pair of
knockers. Postal regula-
tions prohibit showing the
Sheik's knockers, but take
it from me, brother, they're
lovely.

This full-length portrait
shows the Sheik wearing no
top but, staying within the
bounds of decency, wearing
corduroy knickers. Say it;
it's fun. "Nero's nifty
knickers are below his knobby
knockers." Okay, boys and
girls, let's try it now without blowing the candle out.

GETTING BUSTED

A pound of marijuana rolled into cigarettes retails on the market for $630,000.00. All people involved with narcotics and the pushers are extremely wealthy. This can be established by just picking up the paper and looking at the names and addresses of the arrested: waitresses, jazz musicians, fender men, garment center finishers, busboys, dance instructresses. They report these occupations, but they are just subterfuges. Because of the millions of dollars involved with this traffic, these people obviously keep these jobs for a front.

Arrest incidence for marijuana involvements are negligible with most people who have the following occupations: Congressmen, probation officers, bowlers, asthmatics, Ku Klux Klan members, Jewish grandmothers, and opium smokers.

THE HEAT

In user's vulgate, narcotics agents are referred to as "heat." Officers must employ ingenious masquerades, disguises that will allay suspicion.

Disguise I: "The Jumbo"
Appropriate when a twelve-man raid is necessary--one man in the trunk, one in each leg, and one in the body. This subterfuge is extremely successful, since the officers can peek out from the available elephant apertures. The lookout position of the two front eyes is most popular with authorities. The less desirable point-of-view is referred to by special agents as "detail."

Special Officer Frank Lewis
has had 3,150 successful arrests with this disguise--a
female child's torso with
male adult legs. Mr. Lewis
has baffled institutions
such as the Mayo Clinic and
staffers at Johns Hopkins.

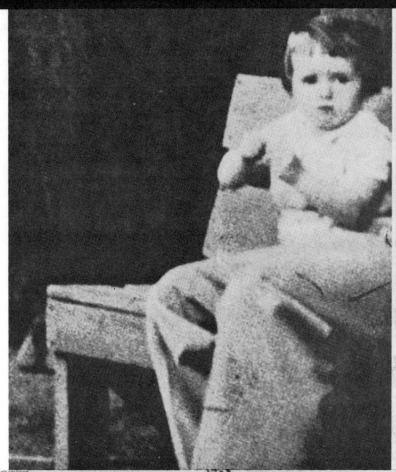

M.R. LEWIS

Here shown sunning himself
at Hyannisport. Mr. Lewis
is a member of the First
Orgonon Institute, Rangeley,
Maine.

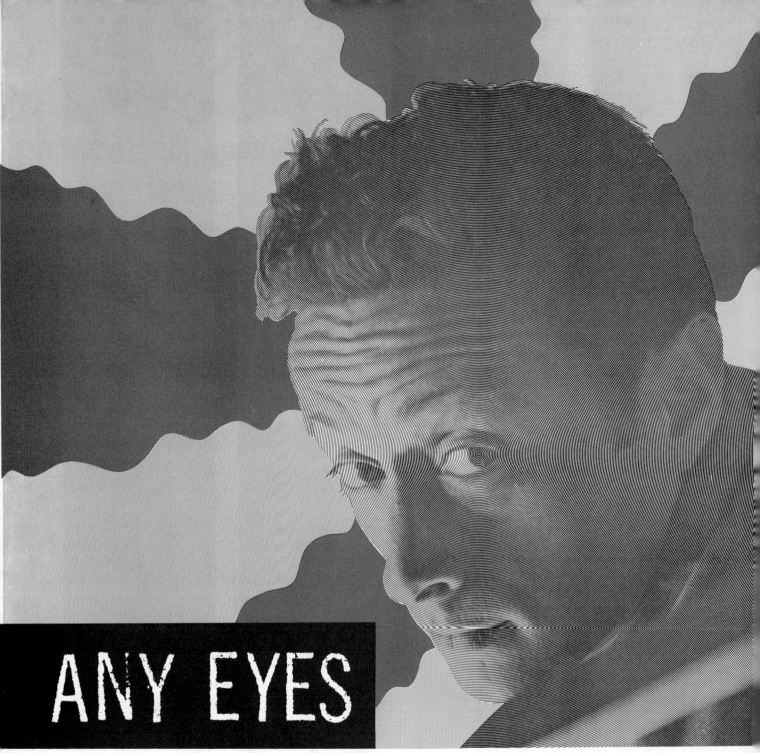

ANY EYES

Look in the suspect's eyes. Hold a flashlight
directly into the iris or, if no flashlight is
available, have the suspect stand on a highway,
and as headlights of oncoming cars flash against
his eyes, suspect makes comments such as "I've
got no eyes to stay here." He's usually guilty.
The term, "I ain't got no eyes" or, "Do you
have eyes?" comes from the drug user's rebellion
against form; in this case, academics satirizing
the "Can I/May I" conflict. "Can I have some
eyes?" "Of course you _can_, if you are able to."
The correct use is, "_May I_ have some eyes?"

JURY DELIBERATION

(The State requests maximum sentence
for the accused, charged with possession of marijuana.)

PUBLIC DEFENDER

Your Honor, I make a motion that the
Prosecution's statement, "Was involved
and did encourage others to partake in
this immoral, degenerate practice" be
stricken from the record. The word
"immoral" is entirely subjective and
not specific.

JUDGE

Objection overruled. Existing stat-
utes give this word, in the context
used, legal credence. Can counsellor
refer to an existing statute that la-
bels marijuana users moralists?

PUBLIC DEFENDER

Which moralist are we using as crite-
ria--Sherman Adams, Bernard Goldfine,
Earl Long, Mayor Jimmy Walker, Huey
Long, William O'Dwyer? Or does the
Court refer to the moralists that violated Federal law: segregationists,
traitorous anarchists who have given
ambiguity to the aphorism "Of the
people, for the people, by the people"?
. . . or the moralists that flouted
Federal law; the bootleg coffers flow-
ing with billions, illegal whiskey drunk
by millions . . . A moral standard
that gives mass criminal rebellion ab-
solution? And in the realm of this
subject, the Defense requests that the
six men on this jury be disqualified
on grounds of unfitness.

JUDGE

Can the Public Defender qualify this
charge?

PUBLIC DEFENDER

The Defense submits these qualitative
and quantitative documents in answer
to the Court's query.

JUDGE
(reads the documents aloud)
". . . And these six jurors have sworn
in the presence of a Notary that their
daily alcoholic consummation, martinis
for lunch and Manhattans before dinner,
totals an average of a half pint per
day. Jurists also stated motivation
for drinking: 'Gives me a lift.'
'Need a boost once in a while.' 'After
a frustrating day at the office, a
couple of belts lifts me out of the
dumps.' " I fail to see the merit in
your plea to disqualify. What is your
point, succinctly?

PUBLIC DEFENDER

"The Mount of Olives" has disappeared
in the moral martini. One cannot cast
the first stone . . . if already stoned.

(DISSOLVE to INTERIOR: JURY ROOM and
new Jurors.)

FIRST WOMAN

You know, I was thinking, that Public
Defender was right. A crutch is a
crutch, no matter if it is made of wood
or aluminum.

SECOND WOMAN

A couple of those jurors gave me the creeps anyway. The one with the thick fingers looked like a real moron.

THIRD WOMAN

And the other one with those sneaky eyes . . . I can always tell a person's character by their eyes.

FIRST WOMAN

To serve on a jury in a civil case is easy, but when you're dealing with drug addicts, it's rough. This damn jury duty has me a nervous wreck. I had to take five sleeping pills to get some rest last night. You build up a tolerance to the damn things so quick. I feel miserable today . . . I'm really draggin'.

SECOND WOMAN

Here, take one of these Dexies.

FIRST WOMAN

What are they for?

SECOND WOMAN

They're amphetamine, Dexedrine span-

sules. My doctor gave them to me for depression and fatigue. They really give you a lift. I take them all the time, except when it's "my time," then I take Demerol.

THIRD WOMAN
(rummaging through her purse and producing a handful of pills:)
Do you know what these red and white ones are? My neighbor's doctor gave them to her to try out. They're supposed to be for nerves. Better than Miltowns.

SECOND WOMAN

Oh, these are Deprol. Umm, no . . . wait a minute . . . I think they're Phenobarbs.

(An ELDERLY WOMAN JUROR, silent until now, turns and speaks:)

ELDERLY WOMAN

Come on, ladies. We need a verdict. What are we going to do with this man?

FIRST WOMAN

Oh, yes . . . the dope addict. How does a person sink that low?

HALO AND GOODBYE

Surprisingly enough, there are psychotics in high public places who have been reported to have sympathetic feelings concerning the stiff penalties the marijuana user and other narcotics offenders receive. I believe, from the newspapers and movies, these people are sick, emotionally immature, degenerates, psychos, unstable. They are not right in the head; so I would assume, if they are weirdos, not right in the head, they belong in jail with all the other crazy people; or do you believe all that crap about mental health programs?

You don't actually believe there are crazy people, do you? You don't actually believe people are emotionally unstable, do you? A person is only bad because he wants to be. You can do anything you want--anything. You can memorize twelve million different 'phone books and all their names--or can you do anything you want?

Or do you believe in the existence of

mental illness, but feel treatment for those ill should be duplexed? Good nuts, the ones that blow up trains with 190 people or repeatedly try to kill themselves, should be sent to Bellevue or other institions equipped with mental health programs. But bad nuts that try to kill themselves with heroin or other narcotics should be sent to jail. What's the sense of sending a narcotics addict to a hospital for intensified therapy and perhaps curing him in three years, when you can have him in and out of jail three times over a period of ten years? Then the last time, you've got him for good. I don't know about you, but I rather enjoy the tax money that is spent to arrest, indict, convict, imprison, parole, and then re-imprison these people. I'd just piss it away on beer anyway.

ARCHEOLOGICAL STROKE BOOKS

Lately, I have been seeing very many serious dissertations on the widespread appeal of the men's magazines. As a reader of almost every male mag, I know I buy them for one good reason--I dig looking at chicks sans clothing. I'm sorry, Parents' Magazine, but I have no big guilts about nudity. A woman's body never looked wicked to me or made me feel dirty. (Passionate, but never sinful.) And I don't need a Kerouac short story or a Rabelaisian Classic for rationalization--I just go for the center girl, and that's it.

Envision a galaxy of blue eyes and rose nipples peeking from the trees and swimming pools that grow in the nebulae of Playboy, Nugget, Rogue, Dude, Pageant (the Legion of Decency's Playboy). All those magazine articles are interspersed with a sweet young Oklahoma ass that is kept from being overexposed by a bulky-knit Italian sweater that never quite does the job; and millions of hips and thighs.

Archeologists a thousand years hence would be confused if these remnants were the only historical data of a populace and its poets, who were waiting for a bomb that never went off. The only thing that was left as a document of this generation was the girlie books. That's all that the archeologists in 9463 found--those intellectual horny books. Their culture seemed to be chiefly concerned with the propagation of their "gods'" wisdom. To date, the names of their gods: Bunny Yeager, Herbert Gold, June Wilkinson; plus a morbid eulogy by Jim Bishop that seemed to be reprinted continually concerning that macabre

day, February 28th, when "They Killed Cash." This odious group has defied all of our scholars' attempts to trace them back to a satisfactory lingual derivation. The insidious subject matter of this essay was superseded by a cartoonlike drawing of an eagle clutching a huge card that read "The Diner's Club" and was signed by one of their most popular gods, John Doe.

This Diner's Club advertisement regularly appeared beside "Bruce Here," Lenny's monthly column in *Rogue* Magazine.

The men and women of this generation were not involved sexually; there are never any children in these magazines. Perhaps they knew sex in a different way then we. The women portrayed are of fine body, and there seems to be no guilt because of nudity, so we assume that they are the predecessors of the Christian aphorism, "God made my body, and if it is dirty, then the imperfection lies with the manufacturer, not the product. Do not remove this tag under penalty of law."

An amazing discovery that has perplexed our scientists is that they never find a trace of pubic hair in any of the photos. Perhaps this is related to the term "fall-out" that is seen continually.

Their comedians were called social commentators. Their label was "sick". The sick comedian followed the healthy comedian, which seems to violate their chronological religious order, "in sickness and in health." Of the sick comedians, the only one we have enough data to report on is a Lenny Bruce. He committed an odious crime: intellectual dishonesty. Upon the realization of his corruption, he killed himself, at the age of 38, in a Hillman Minx. The choice of car was an attempt at death for intellectual honesty. At least he was not paraphrasing the Jimmy Dean "wounded bird" concept. The realization of his corruption came to him many years before his death, but it was not considered truth by his following, since it brought mass indictment.

Lenny Bruce, who professed the desire to help the underdog, with impassioned pleas to spare the life of Chessman, to stop the nuclear testing, to propagate assimilation and thereby evolve integration, to help muscular dystrophy; was in truth, pro-rabies. His was a voice that professed spirituality, but in truth he knew he was a parasite that could be seen with a one-power magnifying glass. His whole structure of success depended on poverty and despair--like J. Edgar Hoover, Jonas Salk, and Jesus Christ. Like the trustees, wardens, death-house maintenance men, millions of policemen, secretaries, uniform-makers, court recorders, criminal court judges, probation officers and district attorneys, whose children joyously unwrap Xmas presents under the tree bought with money earned by keeping men from seeing their child's face beam at a cotton angel; who would have been without jobs if no one in the world had ever violated the law. Like the Owl-Rexall-Thrifty Drugstores, crutchmakers, neurological surgeons, and Parke-Lilly employees on the roof of the Squibb pharmaceutical house, ready to jump because the blind can see, the deaf can hear, the lame can walk. The Messiah has wiped out all diseases, physical and mental.

As the dust gathered on the ambulances, their drivers, and the people that held the moral position of serving humanity, they all nodded in despair that in truth, their very existence, creative ability, and status symbols depended wholly upon poverty, despair, and intellectual dishonesty; and there is no anonymous giver, except maybe the guy who knocks up your daughter.

Other works by the author:

How I Turned a Two-Dollar Smut into a
Statistic For the U.S. Health Department and Brought
Disgrace, Rheumatism, and Blindness to my Family

A LETTER
TO JACK CARTER

Lenny Bruce
c/o Grush Co.
9460 Wilshire Blvd.
Beverly Hills, Calif.
February 1, 1961

QUOTE FROM JACK CARTER INTERVIEW
New York Sunday News 1/29/61
T.V. ALLEY TELLS ME
"Lenny Bruce? Those are fighting words to comedian Jack Carter. 'I think the guy should be stopped by the union from working,' says Carter bitterly. 'The sick comic's embarrassing to the business. He gets up there mouthing four-letter words of filth as if no one had ever heard them before. He indulges himself. His act is nothing more than unprofessional rambling.' "

Dear Jack:

Brother! Did that wake me up! A few other people had told me that, but I didn't believe them. The writers charged me $7,500 for that four-letter-word bit, and they swore to God to me that no one ever heard them before. Being a neophyte, I took them at their word and went braggin' all over that I finally had an original piece of material.

I broke it in in Bridgeport, and it went over just swell. Really terrific. But when I worked Milwaukee, a couple of bopsters who were real dopey, probably on benzedrine or that other stuff that they smoke, said, "Why don't you get some new material?" I thought they were talking about my Sophie Tucker "Mr. Segal, Make it Legal" number that I, er, didn't exactly steal from her because I always start out the number with "To one of the greatest performers in show business today," and then I go into her number. I switched the lyrics around the second show to a "Khrushchev needs a good piece well-laid plan" bit.

Sometimes I'll switch off and use one of Joe E. Lewis's numbers if I find the vice aren't in.

But those guys were talking about my four-letter-word bit. I said, "Are you kidding? You mean to tell me you've heard those words before?" And they said, "Sure." "Where from?" "Oh, from my father, from my uncle." "Well, you'd better tell your father and your uncle that I paid $7,500 for that bit," and do you know that one of those guys just looked at me and said: "Fuck you!" And I said, "I just gave a guy a $1,500 retainer on that bit."

Now Jack, please tell me the truth. Have you ever heard of "Fuck you" before? Tell me, because I'm not going to spend a lot of money on material that people have heard before.

Love,

Lenny
The Rambler

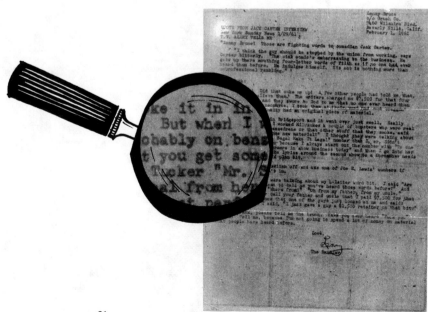

Now See What You've Done?
You've Lost My Place

The chances of anyone reading a book or magazine on a public means of transportation without some sort of interruption are as slim as the Legion of Decency presenting Margaret Sanger with an award for an article on "Making Birth Control Retroactive."

Most interruptions on a plane, bus, or train are caused by strangers sitting next to you. If we are interrupted by our kin, there's no problem, censuring them. For those under fifteen, violence is excellent. Over fifteen depends on the weight and physical condition of your loved ones. If your reading *is* interrupted, here are some tips on how to stop the talkers.

But first you have to learn to tell the difference between sincere people who ask "What time is it?", get an answer and leave it at that, and the kind who ask "What time is it?", you tell them "7:30" and then they say . . . "You sound like you come from Boston." (You nod.) "The way you said 'thirty' . . . " (You nod again.) "I was in the Navy with a kid from Boston." (You *hmmmm*.) "In fact he looked something like you . . . but" (You nod and *hmmmm*.) ". . . he was Jewish." (You cross yourself.) "You're not Jewish" (You erase yourself.) ". . . are you?" (You flash your *Watchtower*.) "No offense . . . you like stories? There's the one about . . . "

To the unsophisticated, one would think ignoring these people would be enough to discourage them. That's not it. A cute trick is . . . blowing your nose in your fingers. Or . . . "Do you smoke pot? It helps me to go to sleep."

When *she* asks "What time is it?", and supposing she is elderly, then you say, "It's time you and I started to relax. I don't know if you know it or not . . . but . . . I've been having a helluva time keeping my hands off of you. That 'Burnt Wisteria Sachet' you're wearing reminds me of my grandmother. She was the only one that understood me. She wasn't narrow-minded like the rest of the family . . . After grandpa passed away . . . you see . . . all his life he had a steel plate in his head. When he was a kid, he used to walk down the street in the real tough ghetto section of South Dakota and all the bullies would sit on the rooftops holding big magnets tied on a piece of rope. They would just lower them and jerk him clean up to the roof!!! Then they would drop him!! It sure was hard on his feet . . .He never had much trouble with dandruff . . . a lot of rust, tho."

A few stories like these and you'd be surprised how sometimes you can clear a whole area. Another cure is to read stories that have little continuity, so when you're interrupted it doesn't matter. I shall show you an example of this in the following story. There will be a place in the story which you can jump to if you are interrupted and it won't matter.

Some guys always get places early. Like me. My plane leaves at 6 A.M. So I decide to shave at the airport.

It's 5:27 A.M. and I've finished shaving. Only the men's room attendant wasn't there when I started. Have you ever shaved with green tincture soap? If you've forgotten it, you used to use it in school. It doesn't make a lather, it just makes about 10 or 12 bubbles. It's the same kind of shave you get when you stay over at some chick's pad and end up shaving with soap. Your face gets all hacked up.

Anyway, that's the kind of shave I got at the Airport. My face was hacked and I needed some toilet paper for the nicks. I tried the door that had the toilet paper but, for the grace of the manufacturer, it could have been a thousand dollar bill or a love letter to Ava Gardner . . . toilet paper, it was in there but I didn't have any change to get in. I felt adventurous. I had my head and shoulders under the door of the toilet when I heard a cough. I looked up at a fat, jolly, red face framed by bare knees and size 48 Boxer shorts. I fell as I crawled out

from under the door. My knees were grimy with dust. I stood facing about twenty guys who were staring at me. They must have entered in that split second that I crawled under the door. "I was trying to get some paper . . . for the cuts . . ." They just sort of edged away from me as I brushed off my knees. My jolly jowled friend came out. "I've seen you somewhere before. Was it under a bed in Pittsburgh or on your knees in a toilet in Toledo?"

(IF YOU ARE INTERRUPTED, THIS IS THE PART OF THE STORY YOU WOULD JUMP TO. THESE INTERRUPTED PIECES MUST NOT FOLLOW THE CONTINUITY OF THE STORY BUT MUST HAVE THE SAME THEME, SO THAT THE READER ISN'T JARRED.)

Guarding a group of the most vicious hardened gangsters across the country wasn't going to be any picnic. Staying up for a week and a half wasn't the problem—I had done that before. The thing that bothered me was going to the toilet and still watching my prisoners. It meant the supreme sacrifice, not only on my part but on the part of the other passengers. I had to go to the toilet with the door open. No one could know I was guarding these men. I couldn't explain to them why I was sitting there with the door open.

I turned to Dirk Redsell, chief of Internal Confidence, who had put the chains on Pick Yokima, the most vicious killer of the century. His handcuffs were chained to his leg cuffs with a neckcuff linking them all together. "Take those chains off that man!" I barked to Dirk. He replied hotly, "I'm not taking orders from anyone sitting on the toilet!"

"I don't want no favors from you, copper!" yelled Ice Pick. I leaped from my seat and with one powerful, short jab, flattened Ice Pick. He looked up ruefully. "I won't forget that, copper!"

I knew Dirk was against me. He was writing a report to Washington, and I managed to get a glimpse of it: ". . . hitting a prisoner without first washing his hands."

There was no one to prove my innocence. I ran to Gate 16 and boarded Pan Am Flight 354, then departing.

We were in the air twelve minutes when I heard a drunk yelling. I looked out the window and to my horror a drunk was holding onto the wing. I tried to get the stewardess' attention, but she was busy counting the gum. The drunk was holding on for dear life. He had a good grip, though. I knew the only way to save his life was to get someone's attention. I started off with an impression of Al Jolson and finished off with my whistling. Everybody applauded including the drunk who, unfortunately, forgot he was holding on.

I turned down Jerry Geisler's offer to defend me. I would have loved to have had him, but I had a loose denture and lisped. And every time I tried to say "Get me Geisler!" I bit my tongue. (Try it sometime.)

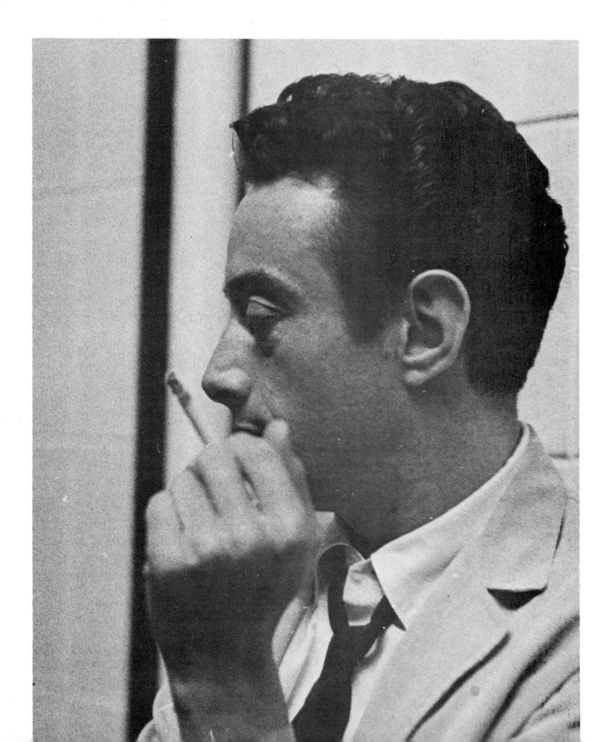

Stream of Consciousness

This piece appeared in the June 1961 issue of *The Realist* . According to Editor Paul Krassner, "While vacationing in Puerto Rico this month between bookings in New York and Chicago, Lenny Bruce sent us the following stream of consciousness. He also enclosed a note saying, 'I love Puerto Rico. Today I went to the refinery and saw cane crushed. Tomorrow I'm going to the busboy plant.'"

Dave Garroway called Betsy Palmer pretentious and righteous. Betsy cooled it because he just lost his wife to "Take one before bedtime and one before each meal" and "Pat, don't rub, the infected area once every four hours for pain," and "Keep in a high place out of reach of children" (Christ, even to kill yourself, you need an I.D.) and "For external use only."

A diaphragm for external use only—that's *really* a preventative measure: wear it outside.

"I can't help it if you put twelve million in the wrong box, the one that says, 'For external use only.' *Sell* 'em that way. Why, it would cost a mint; we would be bankrupt before the nine millionth box . . . Of *course* we'll sell 'em this way, you idiot. Jesus, Mary, and Joseph, I don't know what the hell you would do if you ever had to make a decision. And I don't wanna hear all that Vance Packard market-research crap like 'It has to have a function.' Its function is the most subtle support, ever, of Catholicism and the philosophy it embraces. We are a fifth column undermining birth control. Put them in the wrong boxes. Change the prices. . . ."

A man slimeys up to the counter.
"Three Ramses, please."
"Yes, sir, will there be anything else?"
"No, that's it. Here."
"That's a 'one,' sir."
"Don't tell me they have a tax on safes now?"
"No, the price has gone up—$2.50 for three. . . ."

90

"It's a balloon, Ronnie. Why did Grandma slap me for playing with it? 'Cause they're my Daddy's balloons?"

"It's not a balloon."

"Yes it is. My father would never lie to me, because my father said there is nothing worse than a liar."

"Lenny thinks scumbags are balloons! Lenny's a dumbbell! Ha, ha, Lenny's a dum-dum, Lenny's a dum-dum. . . ."

"Daddy, would you ever lie to me? . . . Owww! Stop it, I didn't call you a liar, I said . . . Owww!"

"Ralph, that's an eight-year-old boy you're punching. Ralph, will you stop! Oh, you crazy Dago, will you—you're going to kill him, listen—"

"Hey, open up in there, it's the super— come on, open the door. God, if you're not stinking up the halls with those peppers . . ."

Oh, eight and bloodied but happy, dear sweet God, I'm happier than if I won the Rolfast Whitfield Ointment and Name-the-Pony Contest.

My father wasn't lying. Ronald Pritchard, home-room 309, was lying. It was a balloon. It took David Niven around the world in eighty days.

That's why I can't wear the damn things, because—regardless of what the Surgeon General of the U.S. Army says—it's a balloon, and if you want to be a silly ass and put a balloon on your wand, go ahead. But please don't do it in front of me. Have some respect for our father who art in heaven hallowed be thy name thy kinkdom come thy will be done on earth as it is in heaven.

If you're pure, a balloon will take you to Heaven. . . if it's not over five years away, because that's how long they're guaranteed for. Imagine springing a leak while passing Jupiter!

On the Great Debate

Everybody hears what he wants to hear. Like when they were in the heat of the 1960 election campaign, I was with a group who were watching the debate, and all the Nixon fans were saying, "Isn't he making Kennedy look like a jerk?"—and all the Kennedy fans were saying, "Look at him make a jerk out of Nixon." Each group really feels that their man is up there making the other man look like an idiot.

So then I realized that a candidate would have had to have been that blatant—he would have had to have looked at his audience right in the camera and say, "I am corrupt, I am the worst choice you could ever have for President."

And even then his following would say, "Boy, there's an honest man. It takes a big guy to admit that. That's the kind of man we should have for a President."

Snobbery Small Talk —A Quiz

"Rejoice, we conquer!" This succinct quotation epitomizes classic verbal snobbery. But Pheideppides, the athlete who ran 20 miles to Athens to report the Greek victory at Marathon, could easily have lost his snobbish standing and been caught in the ponderous trap of oratory, e.g. "I've been running for days. I'm not complaining, mind you. The way I feel about it if a guy's got a job to do, he should do it. Some guys are lazy. I wish I could be that kind of a guy. I just can't. It's not in me. I could have had someone else run, but I always say, if you want to get a job done, you should do it yourself. I could complain and I'll admit I felt sorry for myself running all those miles. I kept complaining my feet are killing me until I saw a man who had no hair. It's dangerous to wash your hair more than once a month. I heard that they've got a pill that will prevent baldness, but the people who make toupées keep it from being put on the market. But listen, what's the difference if you're bald, as long as you've got a good heart?"

Pheideppides obviously was no dullard. If you did not find the above speech saturated with clichés, then apparently you relate in the cliché idiom, so read no further and turn to the center girl and the cartoons. If you found at least one or two clichés, then there is hope.

Complete the test below. I devised this test to assist the testee (no such word, you say, and lexicographers agree—but words become words through usage; they have to start somewhere) in determining the snobbery quotient. Make an "L" through the number that you consider the most chic. Put an "R" through the numbers you consider the most gauche. We do not use an "X" since this is cliché.

1.) *In hotel elevator you and elevator operator are alone. Destination 40th floor.*

PASSENGER:

A. Keeping you busy?

B. Hot enough for you?

C. You're a very attractive man and if you have time, I'd like you to stop in my apartment for a drink or two. (*The sex of the passenger determines the degree of snobbery.*)

2.) *In taxicab.*

CONSUMER:

A. Where can a guy have a party in this town? It sure is dead.

B. I'll bet you sure meet some characters late at night.

C. You've got a boil on the back of your neck.

3.) *In barber shop.*

CONSUMER:

A. Look, I'm not trying to tell you how to do your job, but the last guy really screwed up my head.

B. Give me the works.

C. Do you cut your own hair?

D. Your fingers are unusually thick. I assume that you're not a very aesthetic person and from the looks of your haircut, you have no taste. And I'm not your best friend, but I shan't hesitate to tell you that your breath is revolting, so forget the haircut and just give me a shave.

4.) *Sitting with strippers in B joints.*

CONSUMER:

A. How did a kid like you get mixed up in a business like this?

B. I just come here to see the comedians.

C. (*Accompanied by nervous laugh.*) What the hell are we drinking here for? I've got a bottle up in my room—I'd rather give you the money than this clip joint.

D. All you strippers are a little older than the girls I see in magazines. Is this the place where Norman Mailer got the inspiration for *The Naked and the Dead?*

5.) *Watching professional cameraman shooting stills. His fourth hour of shooting and he's losing light.*

OBSERVER:

A. Taking pictures?

B. I've got a little Brownie I'll bet'd make all them gadgets of yours look sick.

C. You make out with all those girls you photograph?

D. (*Speaking from 100 feet away:*) I wonder if he's shooting at 3.5?

6.) *In house of ill repute.*

VENDOR:

A. I never kiss anybody. I save that for my boyfriend.

B. You're really terrific, Mister.

C. What state are you from?

D. After all, we're all whores in one way or another. (*Note:* "One way or another" *relates to degree. Also, we are all killers in one way or another. However, some people kill flies, others take guns and kill people.* "One way or another" *allows too broad a field of reference.*)

E. No.

For answers to the above test, hold magazine up to mirror.

The functions of this type of test—"In-crease Your Word Power," "Psy-choanalysis," "Mirror of Your Mind," "Test Your IQ,"—are all invalid and in-discriminate. The tester takes a position of possessing superior erudite faculties. This is an impossible task, since I am not fa-miliar with the intellect of every reader, nor is any publisher. So there are no an-swers to this test. However, it's rather amusing for me to picture you holding this magazine up to the mirror.

Fang of the North

Five nights ago, I was with a chick named Mona, who didn't put me through first-date begging trauma. Mona is very popular. She gives you all the second-week date privileges the first night. She agrees to all the usual third-night requests, the three most popular being, "Just touch it once," "Look at it," and "If you won't touch it, please just look at it while I touch it."

She would be completely agreeable to all requests, as long as you would complement hers—let her indulge herself, verbally desecrate herself. To listen to her tell you how inferior she was physically; and at the proper time, you would come to her defense.

For example, she would start out with a "I'm no good to myself, no good to the world. There is nothing in the world I want to do, nothing that interests me. I wouldn't even make a good whore."

Then I would Perry Mason it up with, "Don't kid yourself, Mona, you would make a damn good whore!"

"That's a laff! With my ironing-board figure? No keister, no nothin'. Isn't it ridiculous, you have a nicer ass than I do? Why the hell do you need a nice ass for? I have an ass like Gunga Din."

In desperation, I tried to defend her from herself. "You're crazy, Mona, you have a, er. . . nicer ass than Gunga Din. You have an, well, an interesting body."

She grasped the adjective: "Interesting to the Mayo Clinic, but men are fond of titties and asses."

"Well, that just shows how stupid you are. It just so happens that I go for different physical characteristics in a girl, besides jugs. I like a strong chin and feet with character. Why, look at all those moles! Do you realize how different your body is, no interruptions?"

She didn't believe me and proceeded to spend her case Ace.

". . . Ow! Watch your teeth, sweetheart. You're scraping me. Take it easy!"

She glanced up with the Say-it-ain't-so-Joe look. "I told you I was the lowest."

I was losing ground. "Stop saying that, Mona." She was really starting to bug me. How could I get out of here and not be a brute? Faint? No, she was a nurse—she'd catch me. Then I had it—the most ingenious scheme since legal perjury in New York State adultery-divorce cases. If carried off well, a genius stroke of humanitarianism! Her ego would not only be-saved, but permanently bolstered. I'd fake coming! A fake come—a horny hoax.

I uttered a horrible scream, which is good for an opener. "I think I'm going to come . . Oh, baby, I'm arriving! I'm—oh, Lordy, oh oh Lord Lawdy." (That's my "Uncle Tom Come.")

Before she could show her gratitude by swooping and making cabbage salad out of the rest of my joint, I fled to the bathroom, seizing a *Playboy* Magazine on the way. Now to really make it stroke time!

I was all set. I found a page in the magazine that was a stroker's delight, with about five girls all together, sitting at a millionaire's pool. The old bearded man in the chair is the maintenance man. The millionaire is in a sanatorium for alcoholism.

As I lay on the tile floor, it got cold. Oh, I forgot to tell you—that's the only place I enjoy whacking it, is lying on the floor. I can't make it standing up.

Out of the five, lovely Jackie Risswell was the prettiest. "Jackie hails from Montana. When Jackie isn't busy with the volunteer nursing chapter, she's out on the range with brother Phil, pictured 47-22-19. Phil is 47, has a joint 22 inches long, etc. Note how the cattle shy away from him."

You have to be careful your knuckles don't get too scraped up on the tile in case you get carried away. The black-and-white checkered tile is an unsympathetic bed partner. I forgot to lock the door.

After about forty minutes, my date discovered my disappearance. She barged into the bathroom flattening me against the tub in a Bugs Bunny cartoon manner. "What are you doing on the floor?"

"Am I on the floor? Oh, yes, how did I get on the floor?"

"You're—you're—you're—! Look what you're doing! Oh, God Damn, you really don't dig me. I am the epitome of undesirability. Oh, please, at least let me watch. That way, there will be some togetherness. Come back to bed, Lenny, okay?"

I went back to bed with her.

"Oh, Lenny, I must be the lowest. Rather than ball me again, you lay on the bathroom floor, listening to guys grunt as belt buckles hit your forehead, guys pissing in your eye, and you don't have a sty. (*Note to Editor*: I threw in a little poetry.) Oh God, I must be unattractive!"

By this time, I was thoroughly irritated. I asked her if she had any oil. The best she could come up with was a can of A-1 from her Singer sewing machine. I was obsessed. I had to come. My left leg had cramped twice, I was losing consciousness. If only my wrist would hold out!

I had been going for thirty minutes when her two kids came in and kissed her goodbye. I kept a sense of propriety, I kept my hands under the sheet. Her Siamese cat, whose curiosity had been aroused by the erratic percale ghost, caught a vicious uppercut that was unintentional, but nevertheless he stayed cockeyed for months after.

Suddenly I tossed the sheets aside and put a CRASH MOVEMENT into effect. I squeezed my toes, and my ass, in tight as I could.

She hadn't said anything. I was lying beside her. I had my wrist in second, flipped it over to third, and really started cooking, I was so Goddamn hot. "Talk to me, sweetheart, talk to me, talk to me. Does it make you hot to see me whacking it?"

It was really getting good, I could feel it

happening.

Oh God! I was coming. "I'm coming. Oh baby, kiss me, oh baby, talk to me. Please look at it, look at it, talk to me, say something to me, something sweet—"

And she said it. "I didn't know you were left-handed."

This horny statement gave me a cramp in my head. When I came into focus, she was standing over me, eating a peanut butter, jelly, and bologna sandwich with mayonnaise on it.

I looked down to see where and what page of the magazine I came on. Yippee . . . a Winner!!! Bunny Yeager's car, and in the trunk, yet. All over the equipment. Right in the trunk. Hmm, a trunkful, a whole trunkful.

What would Customs say? What would the Customs say about violating the customs? They'd say, "Unjack it, son! Unjack it! Pronto! Uncome!"

I did it. Uncoming is not as difficult as you might think.

"Come on, son. The sooner we get all that orgone energy back to Rangley, the sooner we can all get out of here. He's done it! Uncoming! He has given the August 1952 Playmate June Bilkeson the sight back in her right eye. There it was, stuck to an ad selling a Voghtlander Speedflex 2 mm movie camera . . ."

Mr. Rhineholt, a West German who took the ad, never dreamed Miss Bilkeson would be on the right of his camera ad. 72 horny postmen whacked it through snow and sleet. 1,790 strokers, whackers like myself, sealed his $8,000 ad and made it worthless. The rest of the issue escaped, all except the ones that came to the house sealed by those horny censors—160,000 stuck to oblivion and loading-platform men. Horror of horrors, they caught the head of the art department in West Germany pumping it . . . not on Miss Bilkeson, on the lens of the Voghtland. How damn far out can you get?

Eight years ago, after an indiscriminate whack fest, I closed the magazine, gluing June Bilkeson's eye to the fender of an Aston Martin.

Timmy and Algernon in the Forest

"This is a proposed kiddie album."

(A flute is playing a light melodic theme. A YOUNG BOY'S VOICE, about seven years old, comes over the flute. The voice is TIMMY.)

TIMMY

Uncle Lenny! Uncle Lenny . . . please sing me a story.

(The flute continues.)

LENNY

(Older, Walter-Brennan-sounding voice:)

Er . . . sing you a song? Sing you a story? Be glad to, Timmy. A B C D E F G, H I J K L-M-N-O-P. Q R S T U V W, X Y Z . . .

(There is a simple, original melody that accompanies this.)

TIMMY

(Disgusted:) Oh, that's just the alphabet. It's not a story.

LENNY

(Sings:) It's as simple as the alphabet.

Can't you see?

It's quite as easy

As A, B, C.

The story of Red Riding Hood

And the wolf she met

All use letters of the alphabet.

Just 26 letters

That are familiar to your ear

Tell all the stories that you will ever hear.

TIMMY

Make up a story, using the letters.

LENNY

(*Laughing:*) All right. Once upon a time, there was a little boy named Timmy.

(SOUND: *The child's laughter interrupts the story.*)

He loved his Mommy and his Daddy, and they loved him. The three of them lived in a clean little log house next to the Great Forest. After Timmy would come home from school, he would take off his school clothes and put on his play clothes. He did this because he was very thoughtful of his mother, and did not want to make extra work for her. Timmy helped his father clean the yard and then got on his little mule and rode into the Great Forest to play.

(SOUND: *Donkey's hooves and flute and rhythm section accompany the child's song:*)

TIMMY

I'm off to the forest
Where it's shady, as a rule.
The moss is green and velvet,
The brook is sweet and cool.
I'm off to the forest,
Astride my little mule,
Where the trees are tall and healthy—
I'm off to music school.

(A YOUTHFUL VOICE *cries out to Timmy. It is his cynical eight-year-old friend,* ALGERNON.)

ALGERNON

Hey, Timmy . . . Timmy!

(*The mule's hoofbeats come to a halt and stop.*)

TIMMY

Oh, hello, Algernon. How are you this fine day?

ALGERNON

Oh, all right, I suppose. Where are you going?

TIMMY

Deeper into the forest—to music school.

ALGERNON

(*Sings, accompanied by bass with bow, baritone saxophone, and rhythm section:*)
I hate music. I hate school.
I hate the forest.
It's a home for a fool.
And I hate you,
'Cause you have your own mule.
(*Speaks:*) Do you hate me?

TIMMY

No, I like you, Algernon. You can share my mule with me, if you like. (*Grunting:*) Here, come up. Sit next to me.

(SOUND: *Hoofbeats pick up again.*)

Do you know why you hate music, Algernon?

98

ALGERNON

No. Why?

TIMMY

'Cause you never listen. That's why people hate a lot of things . . . because they don't know about them.

(SOUND: *A tom-tom comes in loud and clear, becoming more intense.*)

ALGERNON

(In a hushed voice:) Why, that beaver is slapping his broad tail on a log, and it sounds like a drum.

(SOUND: *The drum continues, varying in tempo.*)

BEAVER

(Has a low, goofus voice as he sings:)
Many humans think I'm a dilly,
Have no brains, think I'm dumb.
But it's people who are silly
'Cause they can't use their tails
To play a drum.

(SOUND: *32-bar drum solo.*)
They think I'm an animal,
So I'm dumb.
But at least I can use my tail
To play the drum.

TIMMY

That was wonderful, Mr. Beaver.

ALGERNON

Oh, I suppose it was pretty good. But you haven't got a piano.

(UNCLE LENNY'S VOICE *fades in:*)

LENNY

Well, by this time, all the animals in the forest had gathered around. The deer, the rabbits, the chipmunks, the squirrels, the raccoons, the bears, the birds—oh, just everybody was there. They all looked at each other and felt very sad . . . for they didn't have a piano.

ALGERNON

Ha, ha, ha, ha, ha! Not much of a music school, if you haven't got a piano.

LENNY

The poor animals looked at each other and started to think. They knew they loved each other and, if they worked together, they could have one. For if animals, just like people, work together for one goal that's honest, they'll succeed.

BEAVER

Well, first we'll need a frame.

(A DEEP LITERATE VOICE *comes over the scene:*)

VOICE

I shall be your frame.

LENNY

It was the old hollow tree, who nodded his noble head and strained and bent his strong back.

(SOUND: *Wood bending and twisting.*)

He lay down and put out his branches and made a perfect piano frame. All the animals cheered.

(SOUND: *Cheering.*)

ALGERNON

Well, you've got a frame. But you haven't any strings.

(TWO LIGHT VOICES *speak up in unison:*)

VOICES

That's right . . !

ONE VOICE

I will weave the strings,
From thin to wider.
The strings will be the best—
Woven by a spider.

ALGERNON

What'll you do for pedals?

TWO SWEET, GIRLS' VOICES

(In unison:) We will be the pedals
That have delighted your noses.
We will be the pedals—
We, the wild roses.

ANOTHER VOICE

(Chiming in:) And we will bounce off the strings
To make the sound.
We are the mushrooms
That grow from the ground.

LENNY

So the tree, the wild roses, the mushrooms and the spider showed Algernon that *he* was the fool. To play pretty music, working together is the first rule.

ALGERNON

(Still in a sarcastic vein:) Well, it's a cheap little band—
just a piano and the drums.
(Sings:) You don't even have a bass.
This is surely a musical disgrace,
Not to have a bass.
Why, you'll fall on your face.
Just a made-up piano,
And a dopey old beaver
Who plays his tail on a log.
You're all mixed up.
You're all in a fog.

DEEP BASS VOICE

They do have a bass—
To help the piano and the log.

LENNY

"They do have a bass, they do have a bass,"
laughed the big, bass frog.

(SOUND: *Trio does 32-bar tune. All the animals cheer.*)

TIMMY

Come on, Algernon. It's getting dark, and my supper will be
on the table. We better get home.

(SOUND: *Hooves pick up.*)

Aren't they nice, the animal band? I've learned a lot, this
lovely day—that if everybody works together and helps, it's
more fun and (*with emphasis*) you get more done!

ALGERNON

It's getting dark. I'm afraid.

(SOUND: *Owls hooting. Music: bass, with low baritone sax, etc. A WILD,
CACKLING LAUGH comes over the scene. The owls shriek, and the eerie
sounds in echo chamber electrify the forest.*)

TIMMY

Don't be afraid, Algernon.

THE WITCH

(*Starts out with the wild, cackling laugh.*) You'd better be
afraid!

TIMMY

(*Calmly:*) Who are you?

THE WITCH

(*Sings:*) Heh, heh, heh, heh!
I'm the wicked old witch.
I ride on a broom
I steal little boys,
And take them to my room.
I pinch them and scare them,
I'm wicked as can be.
I'm the wicked old witch,
Hee, hee, hee!
(*Her last "hee, hee" is sort of uncertain.*)
Why aren't you scared, little boy? Why aren't you running?

TIMMY

(*Sings:*) Well, my Mommy and Daddy
Love me and they're very smart.
They taught me lessons early
That helped me from the start.
Learning is better
Than earthly riches,
'Cause one thing I learned is,
There *are* no witches!
You never could take me
Away to your room
Because you can't fly
Away on your broom.

101

THE WITCH

Why, of course I can!

TIMMY

Very well, let's see you!

THE WITCH

(Sings:) Well, I'll have to admit
I really can't fly.
That's just a story,
Just a witches' lie.
But be sure of one thing:
Since Noah's Ark,
Children have been afraid
And hated the dark.

TIMMY

The dark? I don't mean to be disrespectful, but that's really quite ignorant. The dark is beautiful. It helps you watch television, the movies, and rests your eyes. The beautiful stars and the moon would be lost without the dark. It helps you get drowsy; the dark helps you nod. God made the light and the dark. How could you be afraid of something created by God? The light helps you work and play, the dark rests your cares away.

ALGERNON

I never thought of it, but to be afraid of the dark has been very dumb on my part. Your Mommy and Daddy must be very smart.

THE WITCH

Heh, heh, heh, heh! I'll think of some way to scare you. How about the policeman, the man in blue. He scares me. Doesn't he you?

TIMMY

(Sings:) If I ever get lost, the thing to do
Is merely walk up to the man in blue.
By our mommies and our daddies, he is paid
So little children needn't be afraid.
You can't be afraid of people
Who are honest and true.
That's why I'm not afraid
Of the man in blue.

THE WITCH

Looks like you're going to put me out of the scare business. Oh, I've got a good one! How about the dentist—and the doctor?

TIMMY

(Sings:) Nothing can hurt like a bad, bad tooth.
A dentist can help you—
That's the truth—
If you go to see him soon enough.
The dentist won't hurt you

Or be a little rough.
When you're chilly and sick and feeling blue,
Call the doctor—that's the thing to do.
To be sick in bed is no good at all
When your friends are outside playing ball.
If you trust your doctor and are not afraid
You'll be the leader in the health parade.

ALGERNON

I'll bet I know one thing you're afraid of.

TIMMY

What's that?

ALGERNON

Your mother and your father.

TIMMY

(Surprised:) No, I'm not afraid of them.
(Sings:) My mother and my father,
I respect them.
I fear no strap or whip
On the shelf above.
I respect my parents,
Since they give me love.
Whether you're afraid
Really depends
On who you trust
To be your friends.

(SOUND: Thunder and lightning and rain crack over the scene.)

THE WITCH

There's something to frighten you—thunder and lightning.

TIMMY

(Sings:) Thunder and lightning
Aren't frightening.
This I can explain,
For with the thunder comes the blessing
Of the gentle rain.
Surely even you must know
The food on which we live
Is fed by the delicious rain
That thunder and the lightning give.

WITCH

Well, little man, you've taught me a lesson.

ALGERNON

Me too, Timmy.

TIMMY

All right, let's all sing, "I'm Not Afraid."

(SONG: "I'm Not Afraid.")

FINIS

MR. CLEAN

Dear Mr. Club-Owner:—

This is about ears—an important appendage to your business and mine. Everyone hears approximately the same physiological way. Individual hearing may differ in degree, but never in kind. You could never hear with your nose. However, the psychological interpretation of what you hear is vastly different in each individual because of mental genetic inheritance, environmental background, and experience.

The study of semantics in relation to the noun "dirty word" has made us aware of the ominous peril of dirty-word impact and the mental block it causes. No word is dirty, but the stimulus it causes in the mind of the beholder can be dirty, perverted, and filthy, if this individual's recall dwells in the area of pornography. For example:

(FADE INTO INTERIOR *of* OFFICE BUILDING. MEDIUM SHOT *of austere offices of the owner of Studebaker Word Research Corporation and* STUD BAKER. STUD BAKER *faces* LENNY BRUCE, *who in turn faces* STUD BAKER. THEY *face each other.*)

STUD

Let's face it.

LENNY

It's easy to say, but we never faced anything like this before.

STUD

I'll do anything to save face.

(THEY *join in singing* "I can't show my face, can't go anyplace, people stop and stare. . ." CUT *to* WINDOW WASHER'S *curious face.*)

WINDOW WASHER

What's your problem?

STUD

We need some new dirty words.

WINDOW WASHER

Is it some new kind of a game?

LENNY

No, we make up all the dirty words and sayings that you see written on men's room walls and scratched on school desks.

WINDOW WASHER

I always thought kids did that.

STUD

No, it's gotten to be quite a big business today. All those committees and groups have a slush fund when they run out of pornography to censure and places of ill repute to investigate. Then they call us for dirty-word slogans.

WINDOW WASHER

I grew up hearing all those words. Possessing intellect, and using that intellect to further my academic background, I formulated the hypothesis that the words were not *dirty*, but the people who spake them were.

(CUT *to* LONG SHOT *of* PAUL PURIST, *a distinguished-looking man, the owner of the building, as* HE ENTERS. MEDIUM SHOT *of* LENNY *and* STUD *as* THEY *look up at* PAUL.)

PAUL PURIST

Good evening, gentlemen. I'm sorry I'm late, but I just came from church, and I had an appointment to look at the American flag. And then I had to scrub myself with lye.

(HE *glances furtively to the left.*)

Who's she? She's new here.

(CLOSE SHOT *of* LOVELY LADY.)

STUD

That's the accountant's wife.

PAUL PURIST

Ha, ha! Nothing like a little variety! You know what they say: "It's a dirty duck that paddles in one hole."

(HE *turns to* LENNY.)

Lenny, we've had a lot of complaints about your using dirty words and four-letter words. Now, we want to book you in a place called Basil Street in New York, and they are looking askance at you because of your use of dirty words.

LENNY

Can I say the word "stink" on the floor?

PAUL PURIST

Naturally.

LENNY

(Groping:) Let's see. What's another word out of the abstract? Can I talk about my body on the stage? Can I say the word "finger"?

PAUL PURIST

What are you trying to do, put me on?

LENNY

Can I put the two words together. . .?

PAUL PURIST

Certainly *not!*

LENNY

(Voice over, softly:) Why not?

PAUL PURIST

Because you know what I mean!

LENNY

No, mister, *you* know what that means, not I.
(A confused look slowly distorts PAUL'S *face.* FADE OUT.)

As a club owner, you can agree to my terms, or leave me dead in an alley. And I am sure that by doing this, you will certainly be a better person than someone who uses a dirty word on the floor. And by this use of physical violence, you will be spiritually superior to the low-life that uses four-letter words on the floor. Because Bugsy Siegel was *Bar mitzvahed,* and I have never been to a *shul,* and I am quite sure that Al Capone made every High Mass.

Does your fear of my playing your room stem from the fact that you read a review in which the critic took offense at my use of dirty words, and you feel my use of this type of material in your room would offend you personally? Or are you afraid that potential customers will read the review and therefore not appear? The paradox to the whole affair is that this kind of review unfortunately *increases* my nightclub draw. "Dirty word" carries the stigma that you yourself subjectively put on it, and I am curious as to your interpretation of what the critic implied.

Respectfully yours,

Lenny Bruce

105

A LETTER TO JOHN BROGAN, ATTORNEY AT LAW

8825 Hollywood Boulevard
Los Angeles 69, California
February 1, 1964

Mr. John Brogan
Attorney at Law
145 State Street
Springfield, Massachusetts

Dear John:

I'm out of money, the tax is late on my house, and the Detroit Board of Censors is telling the owner I can't come in on the March 1st date. . . They keep arresting me for being sick and taking medicine—a non-narcotic, Methedrine. When I was in San Francisco, I had a siege of narcolepsy and I called the hotel doctor and was refused. He told me he didn't want to get involved.

This has happened in several cities. In Miami, I was arrested for possession of insulin needles used for the administration of Methedrine. Dr. Trop had to come to court, and for the third time I was forced to hire counsel to defend myself and received unfavorable press nationwide. At the time of the arrest, the policeman was two blocks from the doctor's office, and the doctor was in. I begged him to verify the medication [was] for syringes that were properly labeled. He refused, based on a strict interpretation of the Penal Code. Apparently he did not read the preamble found in all penal codes.

If you can get a Writ of Prohibition, it'll give me a breather from a few special peace officers who have used our system to suit their personal whim, which I'm sure is motivated by their early religious training—a training that teaches the strong, the odious rich and the wealthy, as opposed to the weak, poor, and honest. Sparse, bare self-sacrifice, self-denial are all descriptions of unreal culture that propagates lies that may be evidenced in our daily lives; *i.e.*, the Secret Service agent who received a medal for risking his life at President Kennedy's assassination site—received the medal, I assume, for the following deeds:

He pushed Mrs. Kennedy back into the car and covered her body with his own—therefore risking his life to aid the President and save the First Lady's life.

Time Magazine showed the very same pictures, but the captions told the typical, self-sacrificing bullshitting story. The picture of her saving her ass scrambling out of the convertible is captioned, in substance, "The President's wife going to get help for her injured husband," and perhaps I could not form a conclusion that this was an untruth if it were not for the compounding of that lie in the next caption that showed the peace officer pushing her back into the car, and that one said she was helping him aboard.

In a culture where their standard is based on lies and truths, their standard is that lies are bad. They lied. The villainous part of the lie is that when other husbands are shot and wives flee so their faces will not be blown away, they will feel guilt that they are not the wife that the President's wife was.

How this relates to the early religious training that rejects medicine, is: If you're a man, you need no "crutch"—your cortisones, your Bistimith and McFarsen's, your plastic surgery . . . If the Lord wanted you to have a straight back and eyes and nose, He would have born you that way; and it's the work of the devil to put chimpanzee kidneys into the stomach of Man and take eyes from the dead.

Coffee, tea, milk, pillows, blankets, martinis, and sweets and scented soaps and all those "crutches" that relate to pleasure, pleasure, pleasure, pleasure are Satan's tools. What right has man to pleasure? A real man sleeps in the woods and wipes his ass with Saran Wrap, and good women douche with lye.

And thus that Moffit Field incident where soldiers were keeling over with spinal meningitis. Sulfa drugs, that had heretofore been considered the panacea by those afflicted and those who cured the afflicted, had failed. Was prayer the answer? I think not. For they found they had been spitting the pills out, and I've been given to understand this is quite a common problem with doctors who receive answers from those persons who spit the pills out, that they "won't fill their bodies full of those poisons, those dangerous drugs." And those mood elevators—if you have any needs at all, you syphilitic weakling, get on your knees, Brother.

The religious person who would be repulsed at reading this, I suggest you get on your knees for your un-Christlike attitude towards one who knows: "Forgive him for he knows. . ."

I can earn a living and I promise I'll give you the first dollar from every two earned, the money I owe you for Nashville, Tennessee and this request for a Federal Writ of Prohibition to keep those brothers clothed in love from killing me in the interest of Justice.

. . . Another arrest, a secret indictment, is coming February 25. Someone told me. I don't know for what, but the next arrest finds me with no bail, no counsel and, at this writing, I have no money for attorneys. And I resist charity. This resistance, I am aware, is because of a behemoth ego, the cause of all my problems.

Very truly yours,

Lenny Bruce

Obscenity, Narcotics, and Me

This article appeared in the March, 1964 issue of *The Realist*.

Who is guilty of my harassment?

It starts with me, who never took any interest in Civics in school, allowed others to handle the important funds while I screwed around; by the time I came back from screwing around and saw that the idiot kids had taken over the lead, I could control myself with intellectual pursuit and a voice in a bipartisan community through newspaper media. Gradually, the bullies bought up the voice, and now, with the exception of a few periodicals, the voice is gone.

Another party comes to the forefront: slick, organized uniforms. You-knee-form. It's time for the masquerade. Go to court and it's "Hey, Lenny, you've got to wear a blue suit and get a haircut."

Why wear a blue suit? So that those who try the facts will not be burdened searching for the felon.

"Which one is he?"

"Don't you know how to spot them? They wear blue suits."

"How about the *real* men in blue?"

"They wear their brown suit that day."

One of the things I got arrested for in Chicago was showing a picture of a girl that was really pretty. I wanted to point out the God-made-the-body paradox of the decent people who would object to that groovy-looking chick.

I could never sit on a jury and put anybody away for *looking*. If I'm dressing and there's that chick across the way—that blue-eyed, pink-nippled, sweet high-ass from Oklahoma—I'm going to look and I'm going to call my *friends* to look.

But, in our society, it's "Pull down the shade"—and charge two bucks to get in.

That's what repression does.

I could not expect to get a jury that did not read a newspaper, and to make sure they were prejudiced and that The People had their side of the story in first, the newspapers saw to it that I glommed the first handicap, the stigma of being arrested. That in itself puts one in an unsavory light.

The jury found me guilty, and the judge sentenced me to a year in jail and $1,000 fine. The appeal on the case is still pending.

I'd like to fight the appeal on the Chicago obscenity rap on a whole different issue. The obscenity law, when everything else boils away, is: Does it appeal to the prurient interest?

I must get you horny—that's what it means.

If I do a *disgusting* show—a show about eating pork—that's not obscene. Although you Jews and vegetarians and Moslems will bitch your asses off, that's my right as an American, to talk about pork, to extol its virtues, to run in front of a synagogue:

"Here's pork! Look at it, rabbi!"

"Get him out of here, he should be arrested—that's disgusting!"

It doesn't matter. That's why the Pilgrims left England, man. If a guy wants to wail with pork, that's his *schtick*.

Or, if I do a *vulgar* show—I sing rock and roll tunes, wear platform shoes, Kitty Kellys with ankle straps—it's not obscene.

No, obscenity has only one meaning: to appeal to the prurient interest. Well, I want to know what's *wrong* with appealing to the prurient interest? I really want them to stand up and tell me that fucking is dirty and no good.

Do you know there are guys in jail for doing it to *chickens?* Bestiality.

Hey, lady, would you get bugged if your husband balled a chicken?

"I was the last one to know!"

"She was only sitting on my lap—I was *feeding* her."

"Oh, sure, you were feeding her. Everybody *told* me what you were doing to her—and on *our* bed."

"It wasn't on the bed, it was over there—"

"What's happened to your chicken? Have you seen your chicken lately? Tell your *chicken* to fix dinner . . ."

Once I was talking to a horse trainer and a jockey. I'm not hip to track people and their life, but this trainer told me how he really loved animals, and to have a horse that's a winner you've got to lock them up all the time. Just keep them a prisoner and box-car them from town to town, and never let them have any fun with other lady horses. It's the lowest. Just keep them so when that race comes, he's a nut! *Whoosh* . . .

The jockey said to me, "You know, Lenny, sometimes in the morning when the light just starts to break through, some of those fillies are so beautiful, they look like pretty ladies. When they've got those fly-sheets on, they look like negligees flying in the wind."

"Oh, yeah? Uh—did you ever—"

"No."

"Because that's very interesting transference there. I can't see any girlie thing in horses. Now tell me the truth—because I know I'd deny it too if I made it with a filly—but I mean, you know, did you ever?"

He said no, he never did, but then he told me a story that really flipped me, about this horse called "I Salute," out of Isaacson Stables. This horse was a big winner—purse after purse—she really had it made, and the season was almost over.

Five o'clock one morning they caught a 50-year-old exercise man with the horse. Naturally, they busted him. The charge: sodomy. They arraigned him, convicted him, and he got a year in the joint.

Now I started thinking—what a hell of a thing to do time for, you know?

"What are you in for?"

"Never mind."

The most ludicrous thing would be making the arrest, I assume. You'd be so embarrassed.

"I, uh, you're under arrest—uh, *ahem*, come out of there!"

110

Or the judge. How could he really get serious with that? "Where's the complaining witness?"

Anyway, the exercise man was in prison, and the horse must've missed him a lot, because she didn't want to race any more. And she never did race again.

The lowest of the low—from both the felon's point of view and the police eye—is the child-molester. But his most heinous crime is simply that he is bereft of the proper dialogue, for if he spoke his lines thusly, he would never be busted:

"C'mere, Ruthie, c'mere to your Uncle Willie, look at those little apples on you, lemme lift you up, she's gonna have to get a bra-*zeer* soon, let your Uncle Willie tickle-ickle-ickle you, rump-bump-bump on the floor, she's getting some hair on her *booger*, tickle-ickle-ickle, watch her wriggle-wiggle-giggle in Uncle Willie's ruddy palm, don't tell Mommy or you'll break the magic charm."

And Uncle Willie's Mason signet ring snags little Ruthie's nylon underthings . . . children don't wear *panties*.

The newspapers said that the late Pope John was being fed intravenously.

"We don't like to do this, Pope, but we've got to take you downtown. Those marks on your arm there—now don't give us any of that horseshit about intravenous feeding—we hear it all the time."

I'm not anti-Catholic or pro-Catholic, but if I *were* Catholic, I'd be quite hostile toward the press. To quote from the Los Angeles *Herald-Examiner:* "Short of a miracle, [Pope John] could be expected to die at any moment." Superstitious people all over the world waited and waited for that miracle, and it never came.

When my trial for the alleged possession of heroin came to court in Los Angeles, I didn't want to take the oath.

"It seems like sort of a mockery to do this," I said. "I don't really care to but I will. I don't mean to be contemptuous of the Court, but—"

The judge interrupted: "I don't understand your thinking in that matter. That is the custom here, and the rule is that you have to take an oath to get on the stand."

Actually, one has the alternative of "affirming" to tell the truth, rather than swearing on the Bible.

The judge continued: "Do you have any objection to it? If it's a mockery, that is your personal opinion. You have a right to your opinion, but that is the way we do it here."

"Yes, sir."

"All right, swear the witness."

The Clerk: "You do solemnly swear to tell the truth, the whole truth, and nothing but the truth in the matter now pending before this Court, so help you God?"

"I will tell the truth."

The jury found me guilty of possession of heroin.

My probation report reads:

". . . [Bruce] states that he is disappointed with the verdict as he was almost positive that he would be found not guilty. He is hopeful that the court will allow him a new trial and exoneration. He says that as a result of all the cases that are out against him, he is receiving much adverse publicity and this is affecting his livelihood. His only desire is to live a law-abiding life and to be left alone."

And they asked my *mother* about me. At my age! It's embarrassing. What else could a mother say:

". . . [My son] is thoroughly devoted to the welfare of his daughter and making a success of himself in the entertainment field. He is considered by many as being a 'genius' and is very talented. Many people harass him because he is not always conventional and speaks his mind."

The Court adjourned criminal proceedings, so that my fate could be decided by a Dept. 95 hearing, the purpose of which, in California, is to decide whether or not you're a drug addict. If the decision is in the affirmative, then instead of two years in jail, you get ten years of compulsory rehabilitation.

"Mr. Bruce, you're lucky, we're going to give you ten years of help."

"I don't deserve it, really, I'm a rotten bastard."

On the night of October 15, 1963, I was in the bathroom of my home, shaving and talking to Paul Krassner, when four police officers showed up on my property. I knew two of them; one, in fact, with whom I was friendly, had testified in court against me—the Trojan that Horse built—the others were loud and out of line. I asked them to leave if they didn't have a search warrant, whereupon one of them took out his gun, saying: "Here's my search warrant."

We talked about the law—rules of evidence, etc.—and after half an hour, they left. It was very depressing.

But I still say there's nobody "picking" on me. Except the ones that don't piss in the sink. But we *all* do! That's the one common denominator to seize upon. Every man reading this has at one time pissed in the sink. I have and I am part every guy in the world; we're all included. I know that Lyndon Johnson has pissed in the sink. I *know* it. He pretended to be washing his hands, but he was pissing in the sink.

Definitely.

Lyndon Johnson could cut Schopenhauer mind-wise but his *sound* chills it for him. The White Southerner gets kicked in the ass once again for his sound.

"Folks, Ah think nuclear fission—"

"Get outa here, *schmuck*, you don't think nothin'."

The bomb, the bomb, oh, thank God for the bomb. The final answer is, "I'll get my brother—the bomb." Out of all the teaching and bullshitting, that's the end answer we have.

Well, it's a little embarrassing. You see, 17,000 students marched on the White House and Lyndon Johnson was left holding the bag.

"Mr. Johnson, we're 17,000 students who have marched from Annapolis, and we demand to see the bomb."

"Ah'd like to see it mahself, son."

"Aw, c'mon, now, let's see the bomb, we're not gonna hurt anybody, just take a few pictures, then we'll protest, and that's it."

"Son, you gonna think this is a lot of horseshit, but there never was a bomb. Them Hebe Hollywood writers made up the idea and they spread it around, and everybody got afraid of this damn bomb story. But there is no bomb. Just something we keep in the White House garage. We spent three million dollars on it, and once we got it started, it just made a lot of noise and smelled up the house, so we haven't fooled with it since."

"Now, wait a minute. You see, I led the March, and I've got 17,000 students that are protesting the bomb. Don't tell me there's no bomb—"

"Son, Ah'd like to help you if Ah could. If Ah had a bomb—"

"But what am I gonna tell those poor kids out there? That there's no bomb?"

"The only thing that did work out was the button."

"What button?"

"The button that the madmen are always gonna push."

"That's what the bomb is—a button?"

"Yes—it's a button."

"Well, goddamit, give me the button, then!"

"Can't do that, son. It's on a Boy Scout's fly. And some time, somewhere, a fag Scoutmaster is gonna blow up the world."

A shakedown try in Philadelphia . . . over a thousand sinks later . . . *many-multi-milligrams* self-injected by disposable syringes that stop up hotel toilets and bring memos from irate managers. . . .

If I am incarcerated in Chino, I am going to study. Yes, and learn to play the cello. I will come out an accomplished cellist—

and just bore the shit out of everyone.

Incidentally, I use the word "shit" in context. It's not obscene as far as narcotics is concerned—that's the Supreme Court ruling on the picture, *The Connection*—in other words, if you shit in your pants and smoke it, you're cool.

Anyone who does anything for pleasure to indulge his selfish soul will surely burn in Hell. The only medicine that's good for you is iodine, because it burns; a stone is lodged in your urinary tract because nature meant it to be there. So re-tie that umbilical cord, snap on your foreskin, and drown in the water bag, 'cause we're havin' a party and the people are nice.

The what-*should*-be never did exist, but people keep trying to live *up* to it. All the what-should-be's just don't exist. There is only what *is*.

And so the figures will never be in, relating to the unspoken confessions of all those criminals who purchase contraceptives unlawfully, and willfully use them for purposes other than the prevention of disease.

I have played Detroit for almost 8 years, and was due to open at The Alamo in March, but when the Detroit Board of Censors learned of this, they wouldn't permit my appearance, depriving me of my rights without a judicial proceeding.

And *Variety*, the Bible of Show Business, refused to accept an ad from me simply stating that I'm available for bookings.

Fighting my "persecution" . . . It's like asking Barry Goldwater to speak at a memorial to send the Rosenberg kids to college; it's like asking attorney James Donavan, "On your way back from trading the prisoners in Cuba, stop off and see if you can get just one more pardon for Morton Sobell." When I think of all the crap that's been happening to me, the thing that keeps me from getting really outraged or hostile at the people involved with perpetrating these acts is—and I'm sure that Caryl Chessman, or perhaps his next-cell murderer who sits waiting to be murdered, felt this, too—the injustice that anyone is subjected to is really quite an *in* matter.

I have just had confirmed the fact that John L. White, the officer who was supposed to have arrested me, is now in the federal penitentiary near Fort Worth, having been found guilty of possession of narcotics. He had been arraigned on the very day he testified against me; he had come from *jail*.

Oh, yes—one more item which may be of interest to you. In June, 1955, Dr. Gore—he who illegally castrated, not one, but, it turns out, two individuals—wrote an article in *Federal Probation*. Its title: "The Antidote for Delinquency: God-Inspired Love."

Pet Vices

I don't smoke, drink excessively—very often—or anything else on that order. My own particular vice is breathing. [Start "deep breathing," pressing alternate thumbs against "off" nostril—during remainder of this bit, breathe more and more deeply and heavily.] *For years, I've had this bronchitis-asthma-sinus thing going, the whole syndrome. It's kind of a package deal. So when I really want to dissipate, what I do—I go to the drugstore and load up on lots of nosedrops, lots of Vicks, Dristan, all those decongestants; and I go* home and de-congest. Just sit there and breathe up a storm! Go out of my mind with all that free air circulating through my head. Completely *wig out!!* [Pause.] No, actually, that's got a basis in fact. If you're familiar with certain Yoga breathing exercises, that's how they used to get high, back around 4000 B.C. Straight air! And the fuzz can't touch you—that's the beautiful part of it! So, everybody take a deep breath, and let's get *stoned!*

The Fecalphiles

This article first appeared in the November 1964 issue of *The Realist*.

As usual, after you get bored with the defense, you start with the prosecution's argument. In the last year and a half, I've done some thinking. First, I'll give you the Model Penal Code for obscenity that has been adopted by all the states except New Mexico:

"Obscene" means that to the average person, applying contemporary standards, the predominant appeal of that matter, taken as a whole, is to prurient interest, *i.e.*, a shameful or morbid interest in nudity, sex, or excretion which goes substantially beyond customary limits of candor in description or representation of such matters and is matter which is utterly without redeeming social importance.

But "prurient" means 1: craving restlessly: ITCHING; 2: lascivious in thought or desire; 3: exciting to lasciviousness (cf. *Webster's 7th New Collegiate Dictionary*, Copyright 1963, G. & C. Merriam Company) and does *not* mean "a shameful or morbid interest in nudity, sex, or excretion."

Most of my friends were unfortunate enough to have had one uncle or relative who had a dirty mind and constantly embarrassed us with stories that seemed to be designed to degrade our bodies by pointing up any display in manners that would never bring praise nor conjure up Da Vincian imagery. Childlike hysteria at pants ripping—and then the audacity to retell these incidents at family gatherings . . . I try to recall the times I have heard these stories from my elders:

"I was in front of all these people and I bent down to pick up this paper I dropped, and—rip-p-p! Boy, was I ever embarrassed! I had on underwear, though." An interesting side issue is that the storyteller places himself in the role of the one who is embarrassed—or who exposed himself, depending on where you are sitting.

Plus word games: making the number 40 into a joke that sounded like "farty," constant "bean jokes." And when any reference was made to the male genitalia, it was a worm that a fish was constantly eating. And sexual relations never included marriage: "Dis guy goes to a whorehouse, see, and he knocks onna door, and the Madam comes out. Dis guy got a rod on . . ." And the story would build, inevitably, to the guy with his ass out the window, defecating, and—" 'Yeah, who's the guy with the big nose smoking the cigar?' "

The ad-lib honors came to the fore as the speaker grabbed someone's 12-year-old sister and kidded her about her lack of —or soon-to-be-appearing—bosom. With whiskey breath, holding his unwelcoming partner, and with more dummy repartee: "We're gonna get married. Yes, sir, she loves her Uncle Alfred. . . ."

The State has interpreted the word "shit" to mean excrement. The prosecution in Illinois, in every city, consistently gives this definition or interpretation of the taboo derogatory phrase that was allegedly obscene. "God damn you!" Do you interpret that phrase the way the prosecution continually interprets these colloquialisms that have the meaning that the words themselves project? Who is there with this power who can command God to condemn persons, especially you, God damn you? "God damn you" is either prefaced or followed by several words that give it a different import: "God damn you, how many times do I have to tell you to pick up your clothes? You make a mess, but I wouldn't trade you for six daughters!"

The point is that the "God damn" is really "Gee whiz." I have never heard it used as a literal phrase. Nor have I heard the word "excrement" in conversation: "If you think you're going to drag all that excrement into the garage and make a mess, you've got another think coming."

For the prosecution to select "excrement" as the definition for "shit" shows a narrow view. They have unjustly arrested me, tried me, sentenced me, and thereby placed a stigma upon me that has stopped all employment I had in Illinois. They have ignored the others in the city of Chicago who violate the law and have been doing so for many years. These persons go much further in the violation of the Code—if going beyond the ordinary limits of candor in description or representation of excrement is to be considered a test, as the State of Illinois states in their argument.

These magic fun shops with their harmless-looking "Welcome Legionnaire Vs. Zebra Zions"—their Frankenstein ghoul party masks and the rubber shrunken heads are, in truth, just "leader" items. One of our operators risked his life to get the following report, which will be filed shortly with the authorities:

On October 17, 1964, at approximately 11:30 P.M., Sergeants Schnecker and Johnson and Deputy Lechner attended location to purchase allegedly obscene objects that had been reported; said information being filed with the Grand Jury. The hereinafter undersigned certifies under the penalty of perjury that, in substance, the following dialogue and action transpired.

Deputy Lechner, being experienced in fecal areas, spoke with a bit of wolverine dung subtly embedded in the corduroy crevice of his sleeve (a curious honor badge among the fecalphiles).

LECHNER
(Humming, grunting, and straining:) These magic games aren't any fun. It's the same old "death penalty." (Part of the esoteric jargon used by the addict when wanting to make a buy. The fecalphiles, in their psychotic rebellion, use the word "shit" only as a hallowed superlative and in its stead, use words and phrases

that apply to a sense of order.) Yes, sir, I remember a fun shoppe back in North Hollywood where they had cute little tricks—

STOREKEEPER

(Interrupting:) Ah, the masks and the hula skirts are for the un-chic, but for the esoteric, how about this, boy? *(From under the counter, he whisks a shimmering sea of fake vomit.)* "Yeaaa, wooo, ahh, ahh, maaa, braah!" *(With incredible phonographic recall, like a phantom possessed, he accompanies the rubber quasi-vomit with the retching sounds that I had heard weeped from bathroom doors set ajar, and splashing out of cars, onto prom formals, onto asphalt roads.)* Does this look like the real barf? Is this great for a million laughs? Put it on your wife's pillow, and then just read this off the paper when you hear her coming—"Yeaaa, wooo, aahhh, ahh, maaa, braah!" Look at those pieces of carrot and tomato, yellow bile—88 cents, tax included. Uncle Sam's gotta get his.

LECHNER

(Grunting, squeezing:) Naa, we just lookin' around. *(Humming:)* Lookin' around, lookin' around for the curly brown. Say, excuse me, Pop, where's the little boy's room?

STOREKEEPER

Where's the little boy's room? *(His peristalsis action freezes. Those are the words that only a few old-time addicts would know about. Not especially "Where's the little boy's room?", but when it's spoken right after humming of "curly brown.")* We haven't got one here. Try the Chinese restau-rant upstairs. *(The old man waits, respiratory process stilled, for the parry that will answer that thrust.)*

LECHNER

Christ, I could go so bad. . . .

JOHNSON

(From the giant pencil, souvenir seashell counter:) Hey, you wanna use my shoe? Or I gotta spare back pocket. *(Johnson, after 17 years of walking the tightrope, 836 arrests and 822 convictions, has discovered that a well-turned phrase spaced with choice silence is most effective in ferreting out the fecalphiles.)*

STOREKEEPER

(Now a smile blesses his face. He gives forth with the onomatopoeia he had learned from the Tilly and Mac books:) Whew! You guys are okay. You're after a little curly brown, aren't you? You know, a guy can't be too careful today. For a minute, I thought you were the heat. You know, they got nothin' else to do but bust ya for sellin' some Bally-Hoo Gag Girl Books, and those guys are so horny that they'd kill their own sister *(substitution of the normally-used colloquialism by placing a natural phenomenon in its stead).* And I haven't made a sale in a year and a half, but for you guys, I'm gonna take a chance. *(Tears streaming down his face as he gracefully unbuckles his pants and deftly reaches into his boxer shorts:)* You want curly brown, you say? Curly brown you're gonna get. Uh, er, um, grr, um, grr. *(A blur of brown barely misses Lechner's cheek, and Schnecker falls from heart seizure as it reaches the nimble hands of Johnson, who throws it to Lechner and back to*

the storekeeper.)

OFFICERS

(Like Victor McCoughlin, David Niven, and Cary Grant as they embrace:) You fooled us. We thought we were gonna get a face full of shit, and it was—

STOREKEEPER

That's right! *(Laughing and crying with his pants down, and his long balls hanging, and the cellophane package raised high.)* It's Doggonit! Fool your friends. Put it on the stairs. Poo-poo. Put it on a pillow, on a rug—

JOHNSON

(A veteran, he sees the rage mounting in Schnecker's eyes and he whispers:) Take it easy, boy, take it easy.

SCHNECKER

That dirty, filthy old bum! When I think of all the kids he's been selling it to who are probably on the stronger stuff now . . . *(Looking with a blank stare down at the crevice-filled corduroy sleeve:)* Kids! It could have been your brother, his sister, tortured, hunting—searching for wolverine shit, and a bastard like this started them off.

STOREKEEPER

Try it, it's fun! Put it on the stairs, put it on the bed—

SCHNECKER

(Explodes:) Kids chasing after the wolverine, the fastest animal in the world. The heartbreaking frustration of this euphoria, from an animal that never eats. Kids just chasing after dreams, living in a soon-it's-gonna-be world! *(Looks straight at the old man.)* You shit-head, you! You rotten shit-head!

STOREKEEPER

(Quivering:) Give me a break, fellas.

Suspect was arrested at location, transported to and booked at the North Alliance Station. The obscene matter was seized and disposed of, pursuant to 311.

The City Attorney's office has filed charges of conspiracy and joint possession charges against the manufacturers of Doggonit, whose premises are located at locations unknown to the plaintiff at present. The defendant made very few statements after Schnecker's outburst and in fact is pleading scienter.

And Count III, possession of latent material, as in undeveloped films depicting liaisons or other pornography: 16 Whoopee cushions were seized and will be blown up in court and displayed.

The academic question will be for the courts to decide about: dropping the last count of fraud, misrepresentation—for the curly brown, the Doggonit, was not bowser hockey. It was that of a *human being* who doesn't deserve that title. Somewhere, perhaps long ago, there was a predecessor who stooped that low.

It is with great reluctance that I relate the above information, fearful that any bit of knowledge I display would demonstrate to the prosecution my involvement with the subject matter. The reason I know it is human fecal matter that was viciously and fraudulently presented to the public to represent canine fecal matter is that the feces has a different look to it.

Again, I state that I have no morbid interest in the difference between cow flop, horse manure, dog turd, snake shit, and fly fleck.

It is the matter that is material.

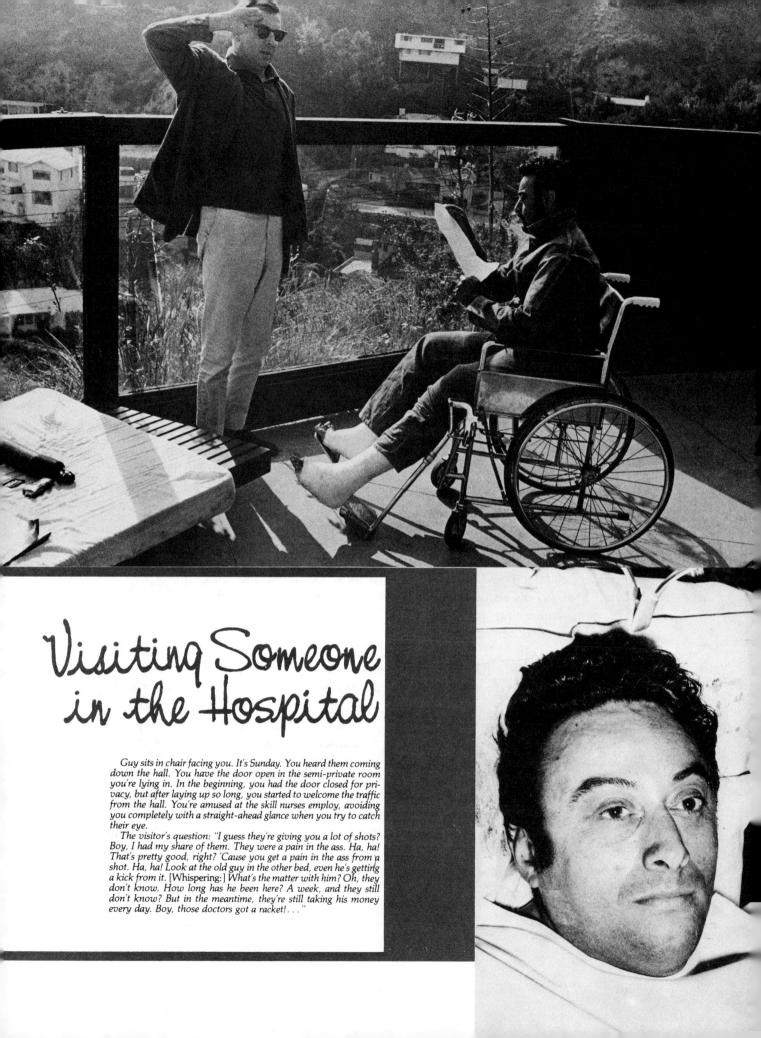

Visiting Someone in the Hospital

Guy sits in chair facing you. It's Sunday. You heard them coming down the hall. You have the door open in the semi-private room you're lying in. In the beginning, you had the door closed for privacy, but after laying up so long, you started to welcome the traffic from the hall. You're amused at the skill nurses employ, avoiding you completely with a straight-ahead glance when you try to catch their eye.

The visitor's question: "I guess they're giving you a lot of shots? Boy, I had my share of them. They were a pain in the ass. Ha, ha! That's pretty good, right? 'Cause you get a pain in the ass from a shot. Ha, ha! Look at the old guy in the other bed, even he's getting a kick from it. [Whispering:] What's the matter with him? Oh, they don't know. How long has he been here? A week, and they still don't know? But in the meantime, they're still taking his money every day. Boy, those doctors got a racket!..."

A GET-WELL LETTER FROM LENNY'S DAUGHTER KITTY

In March of 1965, Lenny Bruce fell from a window in San Francisco's Swiss-American Hotel and suffered two broken ankles.

March 31, 1965

Dear Daddy,

I miss you very much. Since I heard you were sick I got very bugged.

When a person knows their father is working and has't to make a living then its O.K., But when you know that your father is where you are and you can't see him because the hospital doesn't allow children then its very depressing. In the San Francisco Chronicle I read your article about that twentyfive foot fall of yours. I read it over and over and everytime it made me sader and sader. "Grandma says you remind her of Humpty Dumty." In school I am Chairmen of the nervous system, according to my calculations I found you started cursing at the the policemen for a reason, as a reflect action you did so. Because you thought you were getting arrested. That I can understand. You see now your bone will knit together so fine that in a few months you ankel will be ~~hell~~ heeled.

I guess a grandma was getting better She was also getting ready for some action. When you get a little bit better if you think your going up the hill *[to his house]* your wrong, I won't let you. You don't get the proper meals a man should get. and not enough attion so your staying with Grandma and I. Grandma knows a lot about health foods, so with the proper diet you'll be well agin.

Well bring the tape recorder if you want O.K.? I'll see you soon.

~~Lov~~
Love
Kitty Bruce
Love you
get well
soon.

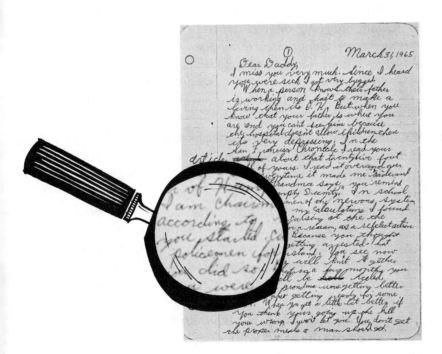

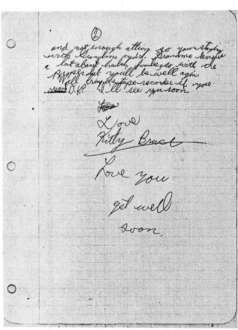

Bruce—He Knows Law; Law Knows Him

This article by Gail Cottman appeared on November 10, 1965 in *College Times*, the student newspaper of California State University at Los Angeles.

I suppose I took too many newspaper articles on Lenny Bruce as gospel, without questioning their validity. To me, Bruce was a neurotic, crude man, over-sexed and catering to the Freudian id present in all of us. I pictured him as a drug addict (although he's never been convicted of the charge), a junkie who built his fame on an iconoclastic attitude toward society, always tearing down and never building up, never placing the best construction on anything.

Now, I realize the stupidity of such a stereotype; of judging a man on the basis of middlemen reports; of believing only the superficial, external presentation of a view and not endeavoring to penetrate below the enamel to discover the motivating core.

Unfortunately, in a brief 30-minute interview, I was unable to discover "what makes Lenny run." Chances are, even if I interviewed him 24 hours a day, I could never figure the man out. He's a human puzzle, a male enigma, as complex as cybernetics and as baffling as the Vietnam crisis.

What I did discover was that the great creator of controversy, the "professional demonstrator," the pride of the vice squad was a humbly perceptive and at times a conservative spokesman who believes his views are of little value to anyone. At times appearing shy and defensive, Bruce was extremely reticent to answer questions of an introspective nature. He admits he believes in nothing tangible or intangible, except himself.

"I'm a gadfly," he said. "I compromise, so actually I have no belief. Rather, I follow what satisfies me and what pleases me and what does me good; and if it doesn't, I compromise with it."

Bruce might be labeled as a legalist, although he abhors classifications of any kind. He has an amazing respect for the law, in spite of his many brushes with it.

He shares little admiration for policemen, although he feels it's "unfair to make him [the policeman] the image of the Gestapo, with a stick in his hand." He's pleased to find a healthy climate dispersing throughout the country—a climate where people no longer allow distinguished Congressmen to be their only voice. Rather, they speak out, protest, demonstrate in an effort to change, to correct what they see wrong.

According to the comedian, the "greatest respect we can have for law and order is to question and challenge the people who are enforcing it." Obviously his respect must be tremendous, since according to Del Kauffman, owner of the Golden Bear where he's currently appearing, a majority of his material pokes questions at laws, especially those of a moral nature.

"The only thing that's immoral is that which is illegal," said Bruce. "That's it. There's nothing immoral that's not illegal. When there's Prohibition, then anybody who drinks is immoral, and any officer should arrest anybody for being immoral—they're being illegal.' The day Prohibition is over, and you can drink, then it's the most moral thing in the world. You're Constitutionally correct to be drunk."

Does he believe there's a higher deity, God, that supersedes laws and the Constitution?

"Certainly not! Since there are four or five gods, I'm never safe. There can't be a higher morality than the law because it's the law of the people, and that's the most moral thing in the world."

Somehow it seems illogical for Bruce, who's been the victim of numerous arrests, to be so staunchly committed to the letter of the law. But he is, and he fails to see how any bad law could ever be passed: "There are no bad laws because every law on the books we agreed on. If we didn't vote on them, then by our omission, we agreed on them. So if it's there, it's ours."

Any problem arising concerning law does not originate in the law itself, but in the enforcer of that law, says the comic. He accuses the police of rendering their own interpretation, when this is the function of the judicial branch: ". . . The cop goes to some member of the judicial branch and he makes a complaint. The judge says, 'O.K., O.K., let's see the will of the people,' and he goes then to the Penal Code—our law—and he sees if there's a violation. If there is no violation, then nothing happens. The trouble with the cop is, he acts independent of the judicial branch. If you would check and see the last time the police department acted against demonstrators, I'll bet they didn't have any warrant to do that."

To enforce his view, he cited an incident occurring recently in San Francisco where the police, without judicial order, broke into television stores and carted away merchandise—the Watts riot in reverse: "They kept an ex-convict in the [police] car, knowing that if they were intercepted, they would say they just arrested the convict with the booty. Then they would let him escape, and all this happens because they didn't have a warrant.

"If you have to go to a member of the judicial branch to get a warrant to investigate when the judicial branch is restricted to the will of the people, then you got the balance; you got the division of power.

". . . Even the judges are afraid of the police. . . . The people are afraid of the police. The *police* are afraid of the police. The police are afraid of the FBI—there's a fear, and their hands have to be slapped."

Bruce might be just the man for the job. He's been in and out of court so often that he's probably on a first-name basis with judges across the country. One judge verbally slapped the comic in *Time* Magazine, saying that "Bruce clearly debased sex and insulted it [and] in his night-club act used unscrubbed words that are common gutter patois for incest, sodomy, and excrement."

Obviously, he denies such charges and finds nothing naughty about his material. Webster's defines "obscene" as "foul; disgusting; offensive to chastity or to modesty," but Bruce simply defines it as "that which has been found obscene in a court of law."

At times, it's difficult to believe his sincerity in expressing this view, but unfortunately there isn't a scale or instrument sensitive enough to measure such abstract vibrations. Nevertheless, as incongruous as it sounds, one must accept the fact that the courts are his criterion for what is and isn't obscene. On an individual level, however, he feels that something is obscene only "if to a person with no more than the average sex instincts of the average man, it places predominant appeal self-demonstrating what it's all about, and is directed to appeal to the prurient interest."

Everyone has a prurient interest, according to Bruce; and when something is dedicated exclusively to it, without any artistic or literary merit, then it borders on the obscene. However, literary circles recognize different standards for judging this.

"The literary view of obscenity is that there's fancy screwing and dirty screwing," said Bruce, "and what's obscene is dirty screwing. In other words, D. H. Lawrence—silk sheets and champagne—that's not obscene. But if you depict a story where two factory workers who are virgins—they don't use contraceptives and they have children, and it's base and vulgar—then it's obscene, which is a completely illiterate view and not the legal view."

He's convinced that the true test of obscenity lies not only in its artistic merit and social importance, but also in the public's acceptance of it: "If the people decide they like it, then it can't be obscene. If they like it, accept it, and go and buy it, obviously its predominant appeal is not to the prurient interest . . . because it is not be-

yond everything the people see.

"In other words, if a lady comes out with nothing on, she's going to appeal to the prurient interest and create a clear and present danger of getting it up, but not getting it off. That's the whole thing—don't get the people horny unless it's going to happen."

Bruce appeared intense and restless as he spoke, frequently shifting around in his chair and fumbling with his hands. He spoke very rapidly, often rambling off incoherent phrases in a voice resembling Marlon Brando in On the Waterfront and a Bronx taxi driver with a bad cold. When asked if he ever said anything on stage that he later regretted, he quietly replied, "No, 'cause I have different kinds of masks . . . I talk to my mother entirely different than I talk to you . . . I talk differently to everybody. If you heard me talking to my daughter, you'd think I was a moron."

As far as his nightclub act is concerned, anything goes, and the public and the police department better be prepared for it. "There can be no prior restraints as far as speech is concerned," he said. "You can't cut off any information. What you consider the foulest, vilest information in the world, you can't cut it off. You can't cut off information about antibiotics, syphilis. You can't do that—it affects the whole strength of the country."

He cited the case of Winters vs. New York in which the Supreme Court ruled that circuses and entertainers are protected by the freedom of the press "because in the propaganda system, what amuses one man educates another. That's where education comes from, and education is the whole strength of the country." Bruce will continue to "educate" the public until "the jury comes in" and the courts, in a unanimous decision, declare his material obscene.

"The wonderful thing is that the jury is given what is called Constitutional fact to try, so what happened was that somewhere in another state, perhaps a guy would have a buck with someone who is making a buck. So somebody says that's obscene. So they take it to the United States Supreme Court, and they say nudity and obscenity are synonymous. They have nothing to do with each other. You could walk around naked all day long, and it's not obscene.

"So that became a Constitutional fact. So what happens is, the jury is given this Constitutional fact; they're given all the other cases tried throughout the country . . . and they must apply these facts upon rules.

"Then it could never be obscene, because no one man can appeal to the prurient interest, 'cause it's a law for ladies—it's a law to protect ladies.

"That's what the whole thing is about. The prurient interest is to men, not to ladies, because ladies have no problems in that area. It's to keep horny guys from getting horny."

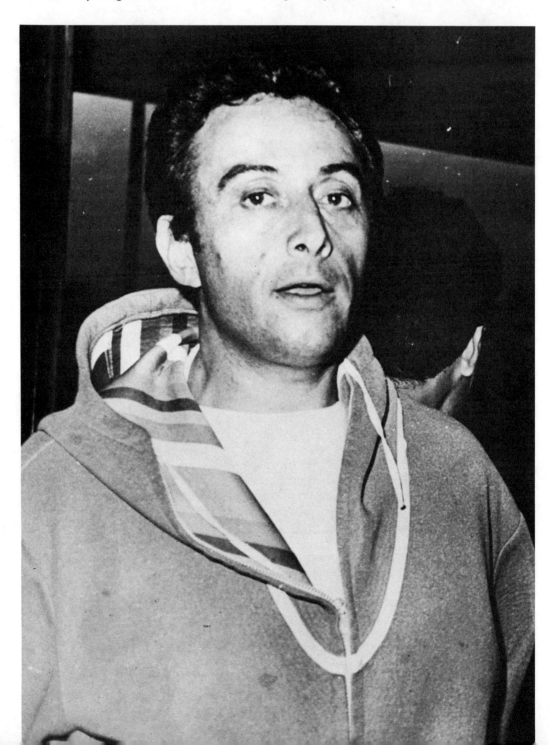

LETTERS TO

RALPH J. GLEASON
c/o
JAZZ
THE
CHRONICLE
SAN FRANCISCO
CALIFORNIA

Dear Ralph
This is our darling Isadore,
that he does not know, as we call him Izzy.
Fine eater, goes thru jars of baby food faster
than you can say gelt. Did we have fun today?
Gave him his first taste of salami, of course
kosher, went wild, would have eaten the whole
roll. Shows what heredity means, his grand-
parents, his mother Becky, and I all love salami.
Got a nice compliment from the Ginsberg Diaper Service,
they say he is above the average. Hope you are eating
good too, and don't worry,
　　　　　　Mommy Pell

Dear Ralph

CARTE

This is our darling Isadore,
that he does not know, as we
call him Izzy. Fine eater goes
thru jars of baby food faster
than you can say gelt. Did we
have fun today? Gave him his
first taste of salami, of course
kosher, went wild, would have
eaten the whole roll. Shows
what heredity means, his grand-
parents, his mother Becky,
and I all love salami. Got a
nice compliment from the
Ginsberg Diaper Service, they
say he is above the average.
Hope you are eating good too,
and don't worry, Mommy Pell

RALPH J. GLEASON
90
JAZZ
THE
CHRONICLE
SAN FRANCISCO
CALIFORNIA

RALPH J. GLEASON

Dear Ralph
  I love you
     Lenny
Here's a *shmuck* who has no concept,
he doesn't type, writes in long hand
but has always rec'd form letters, so figures
that's hip, and sends reviewers them that way. *I.E. . .*

  Hi Mr. Reviewer
    You don't know me,
and my little friend on the
right has been waiting for
you to open this letter
(We realize you're awful
busy writing your column
that we read every day,
but you must hear that
all the time).
    This is our new
"Fantasy Baby"
6011-B.
It's real hep and doing
terrif biz with the R&B psupa
& Sepia market.
You're a great guy
for the work you're doing
and God bless you, buddy
and your family. I have
two sons in the service.
I lost one boy at Iwo
Jima. I knew you'd get a
kick out of that.
      Your Friend
       Tan
     The Record Man—

(Note PSUPA—
   that's colored &
    pseudo-colored)

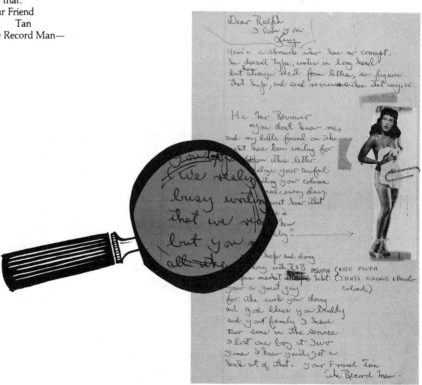

125

An Obituary

by Ralph J. Gleason

There had been rumors before, even the grisly put-on when *The Realist* ran his obituary. But this time, you knew it had to be true. Lenny Bruce was dead.

When the body of Leonard Schneider—stage name Lenny Bruce—was found on the floor of his Hollywood Hills home on August 3, 1966, the Los Angeles police immediately announced that the victim had died of an overdose of a narcotic, probably heroin. The press and TV and radio immediately seized upon this statement and headlined it from coast to coast. The medical report the next day, however, admitted that the cause of death was unknown and the analysis "inconclusive." But, as is the way with the mass media, news grows old, and the truth never quite catches up.

It is fitting that Lenny Bruce should be the victim, in the end, of police malignment and the final irony—being buried with an orthodox Hebrew service, after years of satirizing organized religion.

Lenny was called a "sick comic," though he insisted that society was sick, and not him. He was called a "dirty comic," though he never used a word you and I have not heard since our childhood. His tangles with the law over the use of these words and his arrests on narcotics charges were the only two things that the public really knew about him. Mass media saw to that.

When he was in Mission General Hospital in San Francisco, the hospital announced he had screamed such obscenities that the nurses refused to work in the room with him, so they taped his mouth shut with adhesive tape. The newspapers revelled in this. He was shown on TV, his mouth taped and his eyes rolling in protest, being wheeled into the examining room. Words that nurses never heard? What new phrases he must have invented that day; what priceless epiphanies now forever lost to history!

Lenny Bruce had an incurable disease. He saw through the pretense, hypocrisy, and paradoxes of our society. All he insisted on was that we meet it straight ahead and not cop out or lie about it. "If something about the human body disgusts you," he said, "complain to the manufacturer." He was one of those who, in Hebbel's expression, "have disturbed the world's sleep." And he could not be forgiven.

A San Francisco rock 'n' roll band, The Great Society, wrote a tune about him called "Father Bruce." In it was a line, "The word to kill ain't dirty, but you use a word for lovin', and you end up doin' time." Once, in a particularly poignant discussion of obscenity on stage, Bruce said, "If a titty is pretty, it's dirty; but not if it's bloody and maimed . . . that's why you never see atrocity photos at obscenity trials." He used to point out, too, that the people who watched the killing of the Genovese girl in Queens and who didn't interfere or call a cop would have been quick to do both had a couple been making love. "A true definition of obscenity," he said, "would be to sing about pork outside a synagogue."

Saying this was bad enough, but saying it out loud was unforgivable. "I've been accused of bad taste," Bruce said, "and I'll go down to my grave accused of it and always by the same people—the ones who eat in restaurants that reserve the right to refuse service to anyone." As Shaw pointed out, when you coat your criticism with humor and laughter, you can get away with it. The ultimate joke is to tell the truth while joking. But the trouble with Bruce, as with Chaplin before him, was that he stopped trying to make people laugh. "I'm sorry I haven't been funny," he told the audience at the Jazz Workshop the night he was arrested and came back to the stage after being released. "But I'm not a comedian—I'm Lenny Bruce." And society turned against him, once it realized that he wasn't joking, that he really meant it.

He took on religion, too, by hitting out at religious leaders in his classic "Religions, Inc." There he named names, and this is a country where the big-city police forces are basically Catholic. He stepped on the toes of religion so hard and so often that that two priests who wanted to testify in his behalf in his Chicago trial were ordered—officially or unofficially—not to do so. But they wrote him, and they were his fans.

It was all fair game, open season on everything. Bruce dedicated his autobiography to Jimmy Hoffa, "a true Christian because he hired ex-convicts as, I assume, Christ would have." He talked about Lyndon Johnson having to rehearse how to pronounce "Negro" on TV: "It's *knee*-grow, Lyndon. Come on, try it again—*knee*-grow."

As he became more and more acidulous in his thrusts, *Variety*—which a week earlier had described a Lamb's Club Frolic as "great" but admitted it was "scatalogical"—attacked Bruce as "dirty." It became literally impossible for him to work anywhere outside the cities of New York, Chicago, Miami, Los Angeles, and San Francisco.

Bruce was arrested in Philadelphia for possession of narcotics. The charges were eventually dropped, however, because Bruce had prescriptions for the drugs—and had been offered a deal by a city law enforcement official. Bruce announced the offer, including the price, on TV.

He was arrested in San Francisco within a matter of weeks. Then Chicago. When he returned to San Francisco after his trial and acquittal, there were squad cars around the nightclub like taxis, and the joint was packed with plainclothesmen on the public payroll monitoring the show. They never arrested Bruce in San Francisco a second time, because he was acquitted there. And the *San Francisco Chronicle* supported his right to speak out. But they broke into his hotel room while he was on stage, looking for drugs.

Then they nailed him. Bruce had, said

the arresting officer in Los Angeles, thrown away a matchbook full of heroin. He was jailed for possession. Interestingly enough, the cop who arrested Bruce went to prison himself for smuggling drugs across the border. A columnist who privately agreed once that Bruce might have been framed on his narcotics conviction, and that the case might be broken open if the cop-turned-smuggler angle were publicized, admitted he couldn't lead the crusade, because his paper wouldn't let him.

In Los Angeles, Bruce was repeatedly yanked to the station house and then released—a crude but effective method of stopping his performances. In New York, they found his performance obscene, not on the basis of the performance, but on the testimony of a cop who, on the evidence of the transcript, didn't understand what Bruce was saying. "I get busted for somebody else's act," Lenny kept insisting.

So the last few years were spent in law courts. Most of his time was devoted to reading law. He went broke hiring lawyers (he listed them all on his last album, *Lenny Bruce is Out Again*) and paying for thousands of man-hours of investigation. But he couldn't work with lawyers: lawyers want to make accommodations, and Lenny Bruce wanted vindication.

What was Lenny really like? They've asked me that for years. Well, he was one of the greatest minds I have ever known, so fast it took your breath away. He was a warm, wonderful human being who could write plays for children and loved life and the world.

Was Lenny less funny at the end, choking in the intellectual smog of Los Angeles? He was and he wasn't. Sometimes he was achingly funny; sometimes, deep in the search for some slender logical thread, it was almost as if he forgot the audience. One night he mentioned his father's name and lost the point of the story he was telling. Finally he insisted on going down to the basement to play back the tape he was making, in order to find his place and return to reality.

He was my friend and he died, as Phil Spector said, from "an overdose of police." The earth was pushed over his grave by a tractor. The weekend after he died, Paul Simon dedicated a song to Bruce in the huge arena at Forest Hills, Long Island. "He died from an overdose of hate and bigotry and an underdose of love and understanding," Simon said. Then he sang, "A Most Peculiar Man," a grim song of a lonely death that made a fitting obituary.

But like all truly important people, Lenny Bruce gave so much to the world he can't really leave it. It's just unspeakably sad to know there'll be no more hysterically funny notes in the mail and no more phone calls or mesmerizing shows ending with "Love ya." That's a good ending—Love ya, Lenny. Love ya!